DESTINY OF THE WORLD

DESTINY OF THE WORLD

James Caggianelli

Contents

I want to dedicate this book to my sister, Athena, for
giving me so much inspiration, proving to me that
anything is possible in life. You radiate aliveness and
I'm so proud of you! I also want to dedicate this book to
all the people who have played such a huge part in my
life, you know who you are.
I want to thank the spirits of Albion and all the wisdom
and guidance that the land has given to me over the
years, contributing towards the making of this book. I
am eternally grateful.
And finally, I want to dedicate this book to the divine!

1

chapter

Luca opened his curtains in the morning with one, huge smile on his face. This was a rare sight for somebody about to go to work on a Monday morning. How could he not smile though, when the sun was just peeking over the distant houses and a Robin red- breast was singing its heart out on top of an old oak in his garden, calling to the rest of the town to wake up, it's a new day, a fresh start. Only few would even hear the Robin though, let alone take its advice.

Luca wondered to himself what was actually going on in that little bird's head. How was it so happy, so free of worries, just taking each morning and each day as it came. Why was nature able to do this but humans could not?

He observed the bird for a while longer while pondering over these questions, but was interrupted by his alarm, it was time to get to work.

Luca worked at a nearby garden centre. It was only a part time job but he didn't mind, he loved plants and nature, so why not work at a place you love whilst figuring out what life has planned. At twenty-one years old he was in the perfect place to really listen to his heart and decide what the right path was for him.

He loved going into work every day. He was able to be out in the fresh air taking in nature whilst most others had to be stuck in the sterility of the indoors in a ripe office with eyes fixed on a small screen. What he loved most about working at the garden centre though was that he got to take his time looking after the plants, making sure each one was watered enough, weeded, and got attention equally. This would never be heard of at a normal nine until five where everything has to be done as quickly and efficiently as possible with no time for care or observation about what is actually being done.

There would be no way the office workers got to watch the geese migrate in their ever- changing 'v' formations, or the buzzards and kestrels hover so perfectly in the sky, waiting for the right time to dive down to their victim. He had the time to watch the seasons shift, to shift with them and to respect each season as it came. He flowed with the natural world and admired its simple beauty.

Of course, he still did his job with one hundred percent effort. He took pride in every little job he did, that was just who he was, somebody that did everything to the best of his abilities. Having this attitude would guide him for the rest of his life.

It seemed like a normal day at the garden centre, weeding, listening to bird song, watering the flowers in the early morning sun that were so vibrant that Luca couldn't help but admire them in awe. His attention then swayed from his watering to a conversation between two older women; a conversation that would set his path for the rest of his life.

"I think you are right; you just have to get on with life don't you, I used to work nine until five every single day. I started at eighteen and finished work a couple of years ago at sixty- eight. I didn't particularly like the job but I just got on with it. It is just the way life is. You have to make sure the bills are paid, the mortgage is paid and you have a stable job that pays enough so you can keep that roof over your head."

The other lady then replied: "Exactly, life is about working hard to make sure you have a stable life for your family and one where you know exactly what is coming to you at the exact time so you never get any unpleasant shocks. The last thing you want is changing jobs or risking something just because you are more passionate about some-thing else, and then in the blink of an eye your family is in poverty."

It was an extremely short conversation but was a conversation that struck the very soul of Luca. Just that same morning he was wonder-ing why humans were not as carefree and joyful as the Robin, and now this conversation just triggered something deep within him, it was like the final straw.

'Life is not meant to be this way! It cannot be. There must be a reason why we live this way, this way of life just cannot be what God intended for us.'

The question of 'what is our purpose on Earth' kept swirling around in Luca's head for the rest of the day. One thing was certain for Luca though; the purpose could not be just to work, especially work-ing for a dead- end cause. 'How many people are actually contributing towards a happier, better Earth?' Luca thought, angrily. 'Everybody is just working in a job they hate or at the best find mundane just to pay bills for the house they use to sleep in to then go to work, and a car they then use to guess what, go to work!' 'The purpose cannot be work, sleep, pay bills, get an occasional holiday and repeat, IMPOSSI-BLE!'

He went back to his plants, again, observing them like he did every day; the way each plant had its own uniqueness, a personality of its own. He took note of the colour and the beauty of every one, and the way that every plant was more than just a plant underneath. Each plant was made for a different insect, but at the same time every in-sect was made for the right plant. He saw that even the weeds on the floor were growing little flowers which then lived in service for the tiniest insects, just as the bigger flowers lived in service for the bee and butterfly. It was as if the flower knew of the service it was giving. Every single thing in nature is intelligent, an intelligence that goes far beyond the intellect. This intelligence can only be seen by those who take the time out to observe, as Luca did, every day. Observing is the only way to truly learn, and Luca was only just beginning to find that out.

'Every tree and every plant have so much life,' Luca thought, mesmerized by the simple beauty at the garden centre. 'There must be so much that the plants are doing that we cannot see and do not know about, not just being a life force for humans and other animals.'

He watched a while longer at the crisp, sun- kissed morning. The bees pollinated the flowers and then got energy in return. It was the connection between the bee and the flower where the true magic was. They both needed each other; they both wanted each other. One wouldn't be without the other. This was a type of love, an unconditional love; the most powerful force in the entire universe!

The sun created all this life before his eyes with its energy and life force but worked together with the soil and rain in perfect balance. Luca meditated on the thought that everything in nature worked in perfect harmony. He was truly baffled, and yet customers were walking around like nature was no big deal. They had lost their innerstanding of nature; people had truly forgotten who they were and where they came from. They had forgotten the magic which they were born from. 'All is one!' Luca shouted, unable to control himself. He was starting to innerstand the invisible connection between everything in the universe, but he had only scratched the surface of the truth.

A month flew by but that same question that had been in his head since last month was still there, in fact, it had gotten worse. The thought occupied the majority of his waking hours, unable to control it; but at the same time, he didn't want to control it, he wanted answers; answers to how nature was so perfect and beautiful but yet humans were living the most boring, mundane lives and were settling for it. Humans were settling for the 'facts' that life is mundane, that illness was a part of life, that war was normal, that a life of grinding for no reward was just the way things had to be. He couldn't understand why anybody would believe that their purpose on Earth was to get by with a decent job but never question their true purpose.

It was now December, and the days were as short as they were going to get all year. Sunrise at around eight in the morning and sunset around four in the evening. It meant that hours at work had shrunk, less people wanting to get in the garden during the cold months so it was expected.

Luca now had a fair bit of free time to really think about life, and so one Thursday evening when darkness fell, he decided to take a walk around his local area; a three-mile walk consisting of housing estates, small public footpaths and an odd section of woodland. Normally he took this walk purely to get some fresh air and to think about his own life, admiring how nature worked in perfect synchronicity along the way, but this time was different. This time the walk had a different purpose altogether; to observe it's people. He wanted to find out in detail how the majority of people act, live and behave in the area and then come to the conclusion as to what was going wrong and why people settle for the mundane.

The stars were shining bright as Luca set off, a steady twinkling that put him in an almost trance- like state. The dark made everything seem more mysterious; not scary like many claim, but magical, fairy tale- like. The dark was actually comforting for Luca, he welcomed the power of the night. The stars and the moon seemed like they were watching over him; perhaps they were. He made out Jupiter in the west, and Mars behind it by quite a bit. He had always been interested in the celestial bodies, and when he looked out over them nothing made him feel more connected to himself and the universe in the entire world; it was a feeling he just could not describe. Whilst everybody was inside, even on the cold, winter nights, Luca was outside. He always felt more at home in nature.

As he started walking, houses were full of televisions being watched; nearly every house had a television on, locked away from the real world of nature, separated in their own little brick bubble.

Luca knew there was nothing wrong with television, but when it was watched every single day by every single human that most of the time were consuming the most pointless rubbish, he knew there must be something wrong.

'How can people just sit there and watch programs like that every single day of their lives? They literally have ONE life, and they are wasting it away with programs like that,' he said to himself angrily as he noticed a reality program on somebody's television whilst walking past. 'There is a whole world out there and people just do the same thing day in and day out!'

He carried on his walk, next coming across a group of teenagers smoking some sort of substance.

'So, you have one group of people so lost and so uninspired with life that they have to turn to a television each night to entertain them, and now another group of people that are turning to smoking because existence is apparently so uneventful and dreary that smoking is the only means of excitement in life!'

Now getting more and more annoyed that so many people seemed to be so lost in life, he picked up his pace. 'The world is mad!' he shouted aloud.

He knew though that he should never judge another being for what they were doing, however he saw life for the beauty, the passion and the love for what it really was and couldn't help but get worked up when he saw that so many people were living this ONE life in a way that it was like they were just throwing time away. By ONE life, he meant one life in this physical body as you are now; he knew without a doubt that there was life after death.

Still agitated, he came across a group of friends sat around a campfire singing in a field around one hundred meters from him. They danced, they laughed and seemed genuinely happy, free from drugs and fake news. They were just with friends and nature. This was what Luca was waiting to see. His faith had once again been restored. It was so refreshing after seeing all that negativity to witness something that actually had a true human connection; a connection which was natural, a connection which went much deeper than the material world. They each shared energy and positivity and it made Luca wonder why so few had a pure lifestyle like that.

He stayed there at the entrance gate to the field a while longer and took a glance back at the group he had just seen. They had finished their conversation, now all engrossed on their phones, not one word spoken.

'How come the moment can never last,' Luca thought, confused. 'Why do they think they have to keep checking social media and messages? People always seem to think they must be occupied by an external factor. It seems people can have these moments of connection, but then it never stays, it then fades away back to the world of consuming and distraction. What is wrong with just living in the moment? There is something at play here that is making society act a certain way; it is like nobody knows what to do when they are alone or when a moment passes, or they create a fake good moment like the smokers did, or even distract themselves completely from self with a television each night.'

He had to search for answers; he had to find out what life was meant to be and what was happening to the human race and why.

That night he was woken by a vivid dream. It was a dream of a stunningly beautiful lake glimmering in a fantastic sky-blue colour surrounded by the tallest of mountains, each covered with trees so lush that you would confuse the mountain with the Amazon rainforest. There were all different kinds of birds that were unknown to Luca circling the skies above the mountains, and fishermen were sitting peacefully at the bank of the lake in no rush to catch anything, just living in the moment.

Just before he awoke from the dream, he saw some villagers having dinner underneath a small hut. He saw they were having a selection of home-grown vegetables and fruits including tomatoes, leeks and marrows. They had a huge variety of fish caught from the lake that were being grilled on an open fire, and even a fresh loaf baked by the village women. One of the older villagers, to Luca he looked about eighty, but he could be wrong, saw Luca observing the village's simple, peaceful way of life and said to him: 'So, you want to learn about life, do you?'

That was the end, he then woke up, speechless to the beauty of the setting in his dream. He checked the clock. It was half past three. He had only been asleep about four hours but during that time he felt like he had just gone to heaven and back. He had never dreamt anything like that before in his life.

He awoke once more in the morning after falling back to sleep, but the dream did not continue. Instead, he forgot what he then dreamt in the second part of the night still too taken aback by what he had dreamt of in the first.

He got up, put on his clothes and tried to think about what the dream could mean. 'It surely meant something,' he thought. It felt so real and so powerful to him, it was a feeling he could not put into words.

'The old man knew I was wanting to know about life! He felt so real, I could actually feel his energy, his vibration. He was talking to ME!' Luca thought, utterly astounded by the power of the dream.

Luca was almost certain that a message from great spirit was trying to reach him, and he would be foolish to ignore this dream.

He went downstairs and tried to tell his mother about it, that it felt so incredibly real, like he was really there in the dream. She told him that it sounded amazing, but it was just a dream and to keep on hoping to have the dream again.

It was what his mother said though that caused a bell to go off for Luca; he didn't want to have the dream again. The dream was terrific, it was the most powerful dream he had ever had, but he felt the dream had served its purpose and it had ended at the right time. He felt the message even though he couldn't quite understand what it was yet. All day it was playing on his mind, the beauty of the lake, the mountains as tall and lush as he had ever seen before; but the thing that was on his mind more than anything was the old man. The entire dream was like that man was showing him something and then at the end showed himself, like a big reveal as to who was guiding him in that dream. He seemed to give a message directly to Luca's heart.

'Yes, I do!' Luca shouted, 'I do want to learn about life!'

'Ok,' he thought, 'if it was only a dream then so be it, but if the dream really was an omen, then universe, please give me another sign, an unmistakable sign. There is no rush to give me this sign, but it would mean so much if you could give me a clear message if this dream was truly aimed at me.'

He pondered over how all this began, from questioning the purpose of life and the meaning of existence, to the old women talking about life being made just to work to have a stable income. That then led to more questions and the realisation that life just could not mean that. It was impossible! Finally, the dream occurred, and Luca thought there could be two possible explanations for it. One being because the meaning of life was constantly on his mind and therefore, he dreamt of it, or....

Just as he was about to continue and give his second explanation, a bus came past on the road outside of his window with exactly the same picture of the setting he dreamt about, and at the bottom of the picture in bold capitols it read; VISIT BALI.

Luca could not believe the synchronicity! God had heard. At first it seemed hard to take in, Luca had only heard of Bali before. He opened the computer and looked it up. It was an island of Indonesia, very far away from where he was currently in England, but as soon as he saw the image of his dream on the 2A bus, he knew what he needed to do.

'Bali here I come!' he shouted, looking out to the now empty road where the bus had gone past only a half hour ago and would change his life forever.

That evening Luca sat outside in his back garden with so many emotions running through his being. On one hand he was ecstatic, but on the other hand he had a strong feeling that his life was about to change drastically, and he knew that he was about to step into the unknown. The thing about the unknown though is that you either get frightened off and never experience your full capability, or you face it head on and move towards your destiny. Luca chose the latter with full confidence, even though he was frightened and anxious. It was a good frightened though because he knew that the universe was guiding him and pushing him on the right path one hundred percent. After seeing the sign on the bus, he developed such a strong, comforting, amazing knowing that the universe was always there, watching over him.

Luca wasted no time at all, so the next morning he got up with the sunrise, hailed it like he did every morning and thanked it for showing up on the day he was about to plan his trip to Bali. He then went downstairs, onto the laptop and bought a one- way ticket to Bali. He chose not to go for the return as he had no idea what Bali had in store for him. He would allow fate to decide how long Bali kept him.

The money that he had been saving up from the garden centre he would be using for the trip, but first he would need to convert the money to rupiah. He got his suitcase all packed for his flight on Thursday, two days away. He didn't want to take much, he needed to be free, to be light, not to be brought down by unnecessary possessions. He only would be bringing the essentials, and especially no smartphone, he would not be getting distracted by anything during the trip, this trip was between him and the universe. It was his path, his destiny, his sacred calling.

That was it, he had everything ready, the waiting game was now being played.

The two days dragged on as if they were years, but Thursday morning greeted him at five- fifteen, and it was only just starting to get a little lighter. His family got up with him and gave their farewells, but soon enough he was in the taxi on the way to the airport, a bag of nerves but a great deal more excitement.

Whilst Luca sat on the plane, he began to really feel that he was moving towards his destiny. He was taking a huge leap into unknown territory. The thing about the unknown is that the universe begins to create opportunities left, right and centre, but it is the setting off that is the most difficult part for the majority; but once you set off, as Luca had, a life of mystery, wonder and excitement is created; and once you set off, you cannot turn back!

Luca wondered if for the majority of humankind life was just a cycle. A cycle where the same or very similar things happen each day; an expectation almost as to what is going to happen every day. This creates an extremely mundane life. Not many see the beauty in the simple things, and if they cannot do that, they never will take the bigger steps either. It is about having the courage to break out of the cycle of the 'mundane,' to see the beauty in every tree and every bird song and realise that you yourself have the ability to create your life. Every thought. Every action. Every deed contributes towards the future. The present is where the future is shaped. Once the cycle is broken, life can then be lived to the fullest.

The plane was coming into land and the view outside the window was astounding! Just like in his dream there were mountains that stood so proudly, guarding the land and overlooking the forest and lakes. He had never felt so excited in his life, he felt so free; literally anything could happen, he was surrendering to the flow of life.

He wanted to explore everything and jump out the plane and into the sparkling turquoise lake below, but he could not, the plane carried on until it hit a stop on the runway.

'I will go straight down to that lake later', Luca said to himself, unable to take the beauty of the view out of his mind.

He wasn't sure exactly where he would be staying on the trip, he decided to have a look around first and then pay once he had chosen a place that spoke to him.

After an hour or so of looking around he found a small, welcoming bed and breakfast not far from the lake he saw from the plane. There must have been over a thousand plants in the garden, palm trees, lemon trees and so many more vibrant looking plants that even Luca didn't know what they were. Many were completely different to the ones he worked with at the garden centre back at home, but there were some familiar ones. He noticed that between some of the lush vegetation that kept a small sitting area secluded, there was a flowing stream with the unrivalled peacefulness of the sound of running water. It was something Luca could never explain; just how running water could make him feel so safe and relaxed from anything going on in the outside world. It made him feel so connected to the nature there at his new home, and it was such a warm, magical feeling; a feeling that made him feel so calm and relaxed in both mind and soul. He grabbed a book and sat there listening to the birds that were also unlike anything he had heard before. The colours that surrounded him were mesmerizing, there was not one gap to see out to the town; everywhere was just covered in different plants, it was literally like he was in a world of his own.

He decided that he would go off in search of the lake he saw from the plane window in the fresh air of the morning. For now, he would just ground himself to the new country and the new time zone by watching the incredible sunset, the rays emphasising every plant and colour, and by taking off his shoes and going barefoot, connecting to the electromagnetic Earth below him. He knew how important being grounded and connected to the Earth was, so he just sat with his diary, feet up and breathed in the moment.

The next day he woke ready for his first full day in Bali. He had a peaceful sleep once he finally fell asleep, the excitement keeping him awake for a couple of hours. He opened the curtains eager to see what the weather was like. It was sunny, not one cloud in the sky, exactly how he envisioned it. He couldn't help but let out a huge smile. It was his first day in Bali and he was free to do anything he wanted. He had never felt so alive and eager to experience the world.

He managed to get himself a map of the nearby area, and on that map there was only one big lake surrounded by streams, waterfalls, mountains and small villages. It was roughly a fifteen mile walk to the lake so instead of walking he hired a bike and cycled to half the time of getting there, but still enjoy the journey at a leisurely pace.

He took his time, observing the country and its people who already seemed so much more connected and friendly to their neighbours than the English back at home, who seemed to live very separate, disconnected lives. It seemed to Luca that the less material things people have, the more time they have for human relationships and connections. The people of Bali had more time for the things that really mattered. He observed that the locals valued time with loved ones and friends more than anything; they were happy to live in such a beautiful, yet simple place surrounded by nature with the people they love.

Five miles into the trip and the villages slowly vanished replaced by uninhabited countryside. It would have been so easy to get lost if it was not for his map. He felt like an explorer, and he welcomed that feeling.

The warmth of the wind on his face and the sounds of the birds and animals that were unknown to him put into perspective just how much the world can offer you outside of your own front door. Waterfalls and streams were coming into view, giving signs that the lake and mountains were close by. He figured he had only twenty minutes cycle more. He couldn't take his eyes off the lush trees and shrubs that were growing all around him; the whole place just screamed life!

At the end of the road, he saw the mountain, the one that he spotted from the plane. It was easy to tell apart from the others for it was the largest of them, even standing above the few clouds that were gathering. He stared at it for some time taking in the moment and then carried on until he could see the lake through the vast undergrowth.

After locking his bicycle to a tree, he set about on foot to the lake. Once he arrived at the shore of the lake it came to him like a jolt of lightning. The image he was seeing was the same image that he saw in his dream! It was such a strange feeling, but he was so taken aback by the way destiny worked that he had to just stand there in awe. He had to take a moment to re- adjust to the present so he could just take in the beauty of his destiny unfolding before his eyes. Even though he didn't know what it was yet, he could easily see that the universe was holding his hand along the way. He wasn't walking his journey alone.

Just like in his dream he was standing, staring at the magical lake and mountains for so long. Goosebumps appeared on his arms as he was standing in the presence of God, the creator. 'How can anybody refuse the existence of God?' Luca thought to himself, not knowing at all why he seemed to be the only one who felt these strong, connected feelings to source.

Luca really felt that pure love feeling as he stood at the lake. That unconditional love for all things. 'I am awake!' 'I am love!' Luca shouted these words at the top of his voice, his body pulsating with energy higher than he had ever felt before. It was a magnified feeling to what he had always felt in the presence of nature, a feeling that was indescribable. These feelings could never be put into words, they are way beyond the comprehension of language.

'Thank you, God, for everything and helping my destiny unfold,' he spoke aloud.

This experience had shaken his soul and awakened him to a state of pure bliss. He had only the moment. He didn't want to be anywhere else; it was a moment when the Earth became heaven.

After a dip and a swim in the lake, he looked back up to the mountains, and as he looked back down, in the distance at the far end of the lake, he spotted a tiny settlement of small huts. He had failed to notice them before as he was to captivated by the moment, but he had observed them now and felt a push to go over and check them out.

A good fifteen-minute walk around the shore of the lake from where he was, he reached the village. There were only about ten huts, each very simply, but well built, full of character. Even though there were not many huts, there still seemed like there was so much going on. Children played, laughter was heard all around, and the adults were playing cards. He was still observing from a bit of a distance as he did not want anybody to think he was spying on them.

'No,' he thought, 'I will go and have a look and say hello, they may know some English. I am an adventurer, I must see what life is like over there, after all, I have been searching for a while for the purpose of life.'

As he edged closer, he noticed the villagers had stopped playing cards, the children had stopped playing and they were getting ready for dinner.

'Oh my God,' he thought, 'this is the dinner that I saw in my dream!'

They sat down together, praying before they ate. They ate fish, just like in his dream and a selection of fresh vegetables and fruits, combined with a fresh, crispy loaf.

'Ok God, this is so amazing yet so strange! What next, the old man!'

He knew that fate was guiding him so much at the moment. He looked up when he was swimming at just the right place to see the village, and his dream was all coming true. He was amazed by the power of the divine, and synchronicity was working its wonders.

Suddenly, he heard one of the villagers shout something. He had a feeling that if he looked, it would be the old man.

"Hello," he heard somebody say.

'How did they know I was English?' he thought.

He edged closer trying to make out who said it.

"Hello," Luca shouted back, unsure still who had spoken to him.

He looked into one of the huts and a small family who had just finished eating pointed to the same table he had just seen eating earlier. The image again was the same as his dream.

He went closer, feeling as if everybody was watching him, the stranger in their land; but really nobody cared, they got on with their dinner like a stranger walked into their village every day.

He stopped by the table, and there he was, the old man.

'And there it is, that's my whole dream!' Luca thought, his mouth wide open in amazement.

Used to these synchronicities by now, he introduced himself.

"I am Luca, I have come travelling to Bali, I hope I am not disturbing anybody."

"You are welcome here young man, travelling is good for the soul, adventure is important," the old man replied, a voice so calm and tranquil that Luca immediately felt at ease.

"How did you know I was from England?"

"One can sense using intuition; you saw me and this place in your dream, didn't you?"

"How did you know that! That surely cannot be intuition!"

"No, but I dreamt of you coming here; I have anticipated your arrival for some time. This meeting, Luca, has been written since the dawn of time."

The old man paused and so did Luca. He was completely blown away by how important the old man said this meeting was.

Then, the old man said, "So, you want to learn about life, do you?"

"You said that to me in my dream! Everything that happened in my dream has manifested!"

"It happened for a reason, our meeting like I said before has been prophesized; your destiny has led you to me, this is only the beginning of your journey. Meet me one week from now at the foot of the tallest mountain, but first, enjoy Bali!"

2

chapter

Luca had spent a fantastic week living life to the fullest in Bali. He had fulfilled some of his travelling dreams; swimming in infinity pools overlooking forests, hearing the sounds of the birds, watching heavenly sunsets each night, meeting amazing people, and bathing in some of the most fantastic waterfalls fully immersed in nature, allowing his being to soak up all the nourishment. Bali really was an extraordinary place, other worldly really; it just had a completely different atmosphere than anywhere he had ever been before. It seemed he was really starting to find his truest self in Bali.

It was time now though to meet with the old man in the mountains. He set forth, excited to hear what the old man was going to say.

There was much more cloud cover than there had been the previous week, but it definitely made the area seem a lot more mysterious. He had a buzz in his being, a spring in his step and was so excited, feeling as if he was inside his own movie.

He made his way towards the foot of the tallest mountain, the one that he had seen from the plane and his favourite of the mountains. It stood out even more than usual though, perhaps it was because he was anticipating the old man's presence. The old man was sat on the rocks at the shore of the lake, at the foot of the mountain, in deep meditation. Luca did not want to disturb his silence, so he sat down quietly next to him and just gazed out to the lake, taking in its stillness and tranquility. He was wondering at the same time though just how the old man was so close to him, yet his mind seemed so far away.

The old man awoke but still carried on staring out to the lake for another five minutes. Afterwards, Luca was to be given the old man's full attention.

"What were you doing there, you looked so engrossed," Luca asked, eager to learn.

"It is important that one can know their own minds. We need to be able to take our minds away at will, to focus at will and to be able to observe our thoughts through our consciousness. It is important to relax, but at the same time allow energy to flow; this way you can be in control and aware of your thoughts and not the other way around. Do you meditate at all Luca?"

"You could say that I sit down and just observe nature, but other than that I do not."

"Yes Luca, that is a type of meditation. What most people think about meditation is that you just sit there and hum to yourself, but actually it can be anything you want it to be. It could be like you said, observing nature; it could be putting your energy into just one thought, or even just listening to all the sounds you hear around you."

"What type were you doing then?"

"I took my mind far from here let's just say; but no matter which meditation you do, it is important to stay grounded, that is why I spent some time looking at the beauty of the lake afterwards, because this is where we are, right here, right now."

"I think I am going to start to incorporate different types of meditation into my life," Luca said, already learning from the old man.

"An important lesson I am going to give you straight away, Luca, is that we are not thought; thoughts are things we have, but we are consciousness, therefore we can decide to change our thoughts at will if we are conscious of them and innerstand that. We can develop and learn from the 'negative' ones and then let them go if we are aware of them. To live from our hearts is to live from the consciousness, not thought. Thought is language, what were you before you learnt a language; you were consciousness Luca. Thought then becomes a tool to express consciousness in this life; it is a gift is thought, but we need to choose our thoughts wisely. This way, your whole life becomes one big meditation really. This is why meditation is useful, especially a meditation like you do when you observe nature. Meditations like that allow the consciousness to just BE, with little thought, just feeling and connection. A feeling of oneness. This is why we are called Human BEINGS. To spend time with just you and your consciousness and whatever thoughts come, as don't forget, thoughts are an amazing experience, and we would not be human without them. Being conscious of your thoughts is vital when it comes to getting to know your true self. The reason, Luca, why I keep saying innerstand and not understand is because they are completely different words with completely different meanings. To innerstand is to feel something with the very depths of your being, to feel something without doubts. It is heart centred knowledge from your core being, your true self. All happens for a reason Luca, and everything leads towards evolution. Innerstanding comes from a place of acceptance and peace without the rational mind getting involved like it does when we understand something."

They sat down for a while contemplating each other's words. It seemed like the two had already known each other for ages the way they were vibing and interacting. On a spirit level, perhaps they already did, that maybe why they both felt an instant connection.

"I know you really want to find out about our purpose here in this world, but I want to start off by telling you that you are already on the right path, and that you already know a lot more about life than what you think," the old man said, happy with the fact that he already had a knowledgeable apprentice.

"Do you know, I think you are right. Just last week when I came to the lake for the first time, I had this enlightenment where I felt this unconditional love. I also think I have learnt a lot about life and the mystery and wonder of it by being in nature and gazing at the stars constantly back home."

The old man told Luca that what he felt was his true self, and that he could tell he had been connected and awake all his life, but that Bali had really brought out his potential. He also told him that he would just keep on growing, as in life, there are no limits.

"Ok Luca, I like to break down the purpose of life into four main purposes. Number one purpose is to make sure that you live your life to the fullest, gaining each experience that your soul desires.

Number two purpose is to help nature and humanity thrive out of pure of heart.

Number three is to fulfil your own unique destiny, your individual mission here on Earth.

And the final main purpose is to better yourself in some way every day. To evolve, to higher your consciousness, to know thyself. To develop spiritually, physically, and emotionally each day. To expand your soul."

Luca was taken aback by the simplicity of his answer, but it resonated deeply in his heart. He still however had so many questions he wanted to ask!

"What do you mean by humanity's destiny though?"

"The destiny of humanity is to unite into a new level of consciousness, where love and authenticity is the ruler; where we are all once again connected to nature, to Mother Earth."

The old man continued, "God has incarnated himself into separate beings to experience himself through diverse levels of consciousness in this physical plane. This may sound confusing but everything in nature is a unique being, the trees, the animals, humans, and so on. We are all connected to the mother though, which is the Earth itself. The beauty is that every single being and every single human is different. There is so much diversity. Everything has a unique soul yet is still part of that 'God' soul if you know what I mean."

The wise young Luca was already beginning to innerstand this. He had never been so engrossed with what somebody was saying so much before.

"We need to all realise that we are all connected; only then can humanity truly be a community and fulfil its destiny, just like the rest of nature is one, interconnected community. Life is one huge game. One exciting game with emotions, laughter, challenges, obstacles, fears, intense relationships. It truly becomes heaven once you realise who you are as an infinite spiritual being simply having a human experience. I think, Luca, you already reached that pure love feeling before when you came here to the lake. We need to reach a similar state you captured collectively though; only then can we truly be in balance with nature and the human nature within ourselves. The energy is changing in the world and there are tests of the soul left, right and centre at the moment for humanity. Those that are consumed by greed are trying to manipulate humanity, trying to suck their life force and control them forever. They are taking our humanity away. By humanity, I mean our individuality, our connection to Mother Earth. They are ungrounding and distracting us more so than ever before. The creator knows this though; so it is our test to see if we can overcome these challenges and move towards the golden ray of light. It is all part of the divine plan that God set out. It is the most exciting time ever to be alive in this realm. This is going to be the biggest shift in collective consciousness that has ever taken place on Earth."

Luca sat there for a while, looking up at the mountains around him, feeling the stillness of the lake caressing his mind and body, thinking about his words.

"I want you to try something Luca; I want you to look out to the lake and hear the silence. Take in only the beauty of the lake and the moment. Too many people add material things to their lives to make them feel more complete when the key is to feel complete without having anything. To feel comfortable being with just you. We need to take all the noise away, all the meaningless distractions like social media, gossip, news and obsessing negatively about the past or the future. Peace is in the present. To be just you and your consciousness in the present is balance, and balance is the key to all. Of course, we can go on things like the internet at times, but so long as it is in balance, and it does not dictate our lives. Now Luca, focus on the lake and nothing else."

Luca sat for a half hour and only allowed the lake to flow through his mind, taking in all its glory. This exercise allowed Luca to forget everything and to be completely at peace with himself and the world around him. It allowed him to feel a connection and a feeling of oneness to the spirits of the lake.

He listened to the tiny waves that formed at the shore of the lake, taking him into an almost trance- like state. Birds were singing all around him, happy also with the present, and he felt a cool breeze on his face. He breathed in a deep breath, taking in the energy that was there, and gradually allowed his soul to move into a state of bliss. There it was again, that pure love feeling. He could now, as taught by the old man, move into that state at will just by being conscious and taking in the universe.

After the half hour was up, the old man stood up and then threw himself into the lake. Luca followed, and they took in the beauty of Bali together, the freshness of the lake water caressing their bodies.

"You managed to get back that pure love feeling again, didn't you Luca?"

"I did," Luca replied, feeling so peaceful yet simultaneously ecstatic.

"What you did is you increased your state of consciousness and got in touch with your true self. You saw the universe as it really is, full of love and magic. When that happens, it is like you and the world are one and the same. God's eyes are your eyes and vice versa. This is because it is true; God is experiencing himself and looking at his own creation through your eyes and the eyes of all that is in nature. All is one remember! Enlightenment is merely a union between your higher self and human self."

There was a silence each time he spoke as Luca embraced all his wisdom.

"I want to tell you about the ten principles of life, Luca, what I call the ten essentials. I won't go over them in too much detail as I have taught you much today, but they go like this…

Number one is nourishment through food. We should only be eating foods that are natural, from the Earth, be it growing or grazing on the land. The food industry has been corrupted to the core, just like all the other systems. People are eating food- like products, not even real, whole foods! We should be picking our fruit, baking our home-made bread with natural ingredients, and giving our money to local, organic farmers. So many people are buying processed, artificial, and genetically modified food; but then again, it is the level of conscious awareness that is manifesting this. If you are connected and aware of your body, you are going to naturally want good, natural food; it is the disconnection leading people astray. We are natural beings that need natural food. If I buy a bar of chocolate, I only expect it to have raw cocoa and organic sugar, not a thousand ingredients like the shop bought crap has!"

Luca was smiling at the language the old man used and his passion for the subject, but he was spot on with what he was saying.

The old man continued, "It is vital we learn to re- connect with our food. It is one of our sources of life. Let's be thankful to the land that created it, let's enjoy it, not rush it. I go out myself on a sunny day with the sound of bird song and simply slow down and pick my fruit, giving thanks. I then sit and eat it by the lake, acknowledging where it comes from and enjoying the flavours with my God- given senses."

The way the old man had a passion for something as simple as eating inspired Luca on a deep soul level. He was igniting all his senses in the moment, and appreciated what the land has given him.

The old man continued with the essentials…

"Number two is simply a good night's sleep. Sleep is a magical tool to re- charge and re- energise ourselves, mind, body and soul. A lot of the time, if you feel a little run down, just getting a few extra hours sleep can charge the body fully, it is that powerful! Sleep has countless benefits. When we enter our dream state, a lot of the time we enter our subconscious mind. In this state, our subconscious shows us many things that are holding us back, it shows us fears and doubts and what we need to work on. We should treat this as a gift, as then, in the day we can learn to heal from all the things that our dream state showed us. Sometimes, we enter other worlds, and we access our highest, true self. When we experience this in the dream space it can be immensely powerful, sometimes life altering. Sleep is part of life. It is there to serve us.

Number three is drinking pure spring water from the Earth. Sacred springs were once honoured all over the world, but now, modern society has forgot about them. They have been disrespected, built over, demolished, and shut off. So many are still running though, and it is our job to re- introduce them. They have been hidden by the big, corporate water giants so they can make us pay for chemically loaded water and disconnect us from where everything comes from, when spring water is in fact, free, clean, pure, and unlimited! You see, Luca, the truth about water has been hidden in plain sight. Water, in its purest form is primary spring water. Now, most people think that spring water can be found in the local supermarket when that is not the case at all. The water in the shop is ozonated and put though many treatments before it is then sold to us. We should be drinking water straight from the source of a spring, because in its purest form, spring water comes directly from the Earth's womb, and has never been touched by any layer above, that means no man has ever gone near it with all the chemicals that we produce in the poisoned, modern world. It is primary water. This water is being constantly renewed by the Earth. Not from the rain, from the Earth itself! Spring water then flows through layer after layer of sacred crystal over thousands of years, picking up energy, memory, and minerals until it finally reaches the surface where it comes out the springs that the ancients built rocks around to honour the spirits of the water. The ancients knew that everything in life comes from water, one of the main elements; but this knowledge, especially over the last one hundred years has been stripped so they can make us drink the chemically loaded tap water, and ozonated bottled water. It is criminal! There is hope though, Luca, the waters are still running, it is just up to us now to acknowledge this and start re-introducing and drinking from the sacred springs. The old world even used to bathe in the waters! In fact, they used to do this up until the late 1800's, after that, it was phased out. It was not just the 'romans' that had these baths, the entire world did. They knew how important the pure, mineral loaded waters and hot spring baths were for healing the body. I drink from a sacred spring every day, Luca, and even the taste is in a completely different league! This is not to neglect the waters above though. We have the underground waters and the waters we can see. This is why the ancients called them the waters using the plural. The waters above are the streams, rivers and lakes we can see. These are affected by rainwater and the water cycle, and then we have the waters below which are the primary waters. Both are just as important as the other. We have affected the waters above more than anything by destroying the forests, polluting the Earth with chemicals and so on, and this is what dries up and harms the waters we can see. The waters below are unaffected by chemicals as they have never come close to our poisoned layers before, however, spiritually, they are affected as they are energetically connected to the waters above, just like we are energetically connected to all existence. The aim is to once again unite the waters and see them both as sacred.

Luca was fascinated by all this, gaining a new appreciation for what water truly is and where it comes from.

"Wow, I never knew that! That is terrible, why have they hidden the springs and told us lies? Why are they wanting to harm us just for money?"

"I will explain all in good time, Luca, but first I must get back to the essentials."

Luca sat back, thinking about the magnificence of the Earth; how it constantly produces unlimited, clean water for humans and all life. Constantly abundant, constantly giving.

"Number four is meditation and breathing. Meditation is great for calming the mind and identifying thought patterns, and like I said before, learning to be conscious. At least once a day, sit by yourself in the morning or at night and just relax. Get to know yourself. What can you hear, smell, see. Feel the sunlight on your skin, the wind on your face. Feel the aliveness pulsating in your body. Meditation is all about being present, being conscious, and feeling alive. It is the goal of life to live it as one, big meditation! To know thyself is the most important thing, the greatest journey. It is in times of introspection that we learn and feel the most about ourselves and the world around us.

Breathing deeply and consciously is fantastic too. By breathing the air, you are breathing in life, it is as simple as that. Every breath keeps you alive, just think about that, Luca, when you have a moment. Try doing some powerful, conscious breaths throughout the day. Imagine the life force filling you up, cleansing you and healing you. You can also do practices where you just focus on your breath for a while, connecting to what keeps you alive. No matter what happens in life, you always have your breath."

Luca took a deep breath, and let it go through his mouth, his body in such a relaxed state.

"Number five is grounding barefoot to the Earth and sun- gazing. Both of these are powerful practices. Grounding connects our electromagnetic body to the Earth's electromagnetic body. It energises us, as we are electrical, energetic beings too, and by connecting to the Earth's frequency, our bodies then re- balance. There are so many benefits to this. By grounding, we drop our negative energy into the Earth, and pick up the positive electrons from it. We regulate our nervous system, and we calm down any inflammation. We also improve sleep and relaxation, and our senses themselves sharpen. But most importantly, we connect to our mother, the Earth, gaining a relationship with her.

Sun gazing is also such a powerful tool. By getting out and gazing at the sun's rays as soon as it rises and sets so it is not too bright, we connect to the all giving life force that is the sun, that nothing would live without, energising every cell in our being. We connect to our true, circadian rhythm. This makes us feel more grounded, more in tune, more at peace. Again, our state of relaxation improves, and we feel much more connected to the cycle of life. When we acknowledge the sun in this way, we are acknowledging the very thing that creates life, and that created us. It is so powerful!

Number six is movement. Everything moves, it flows. By moving our bodies in a way that feels right to us, and by keeping our bodies strong, fit and loose, we also allow energy to flow through us; we then do not stagnate. We need to flow like the river, not stagnate like a pond. We must pick a movement practice that suits us and stick to it. It could be something as simple as walking, but it could be dancing, playing sport, running; it could be anything. Movement allows us to really connect to our bodies and our breath in the present moment, and when we feel grounded in this way, we can develop some incredible feelings."

Luca agreed with every word he said. All his life he had loved to play sport and move his body, and he felt his best when he was outside on the move.

"It is vital to rest though as well, Luca. We need a balance. To take time out by ourselves and do nothing is so important for our well- being. To take a bath with candles, to read a good book; it is all part of this dance of life.

Number seven is knowing who you are. We do this by spending time with ourselves and listening to what is true in our own hearts; identifying beliefs that are not our own, and doing what we think is right for ourselves. This is why our souls have come down here; to really find what it means to be alive in a body and experience the full spectrum of human emotions and feelings.

Number eight is being in nature. Nature is the divine. All of the divine secrets are in plain sight in nature, not in some forgotten book in a faraway place. Every leaf, every flower, every bird is so beautiful and so unique. Everything comes from the sacred spiral of life. Just look at your fingertips and then a fallen tree trunk, they both have the sacred spiral because we are all connected; but the spiral is always slightly different on everybody, signifying our uniqueness. We are all a part of the divine creator, so being and spending time in the natural world, be it a forest, a lake, the sea, or even your own garden is like coming home to ourselves. The physical, emotional, and spiritual benefits are just extraordinary. By immersing ourselves in nature, we are communicating with all the nature spirits. The ancient world and the aboriginals to this day know that everything in nature has its own spirit, God or Goddess; and each cycle of the nature wheel is ruled by one of these. The Celtic druids for example followed their own nature wheel. They had Imbolc, the first celebration of the year following the depths of winter at the start of February, ruled by the goddess Brigid. She was the fertility goddess. The darkness of winter comes to an end during this time and the first snowdrops and daffodils start to appear. The next celebration is the Spring equinox or Ostara, the day of balance, where night and day are of equal lengths. This is truly the start of spring where things are about to go into full bloom. In between the summer solstice and the spring Equinox is Beltane, the time of year where the greenery is really starting to grow into full force. Next, we have the summer solstice, the point of year where the energy is at its highest point. This is the longest day of the year. After that, the energy starts slowly drawing inwards again, and we have the festival of Lammas, which has always been known as the day that marks the harvest season. Around the twenty- third of September in the northern hemisphere falls the autumn equinox, again a day of balance, and the day that marks the start of autumn. Finally, it is the winter solstice, the shortest day of the year, and the time the energy is at a low point for the year, a time for great introspection. After that, the wheel starts again with Imbolc. They followed this cycle to connect and stay in tune with the cycles of the Earth. It was a way of life. They followed the waxing and waning of the moon also and had festivities to mark the full and new moons. All these ceremonies were lost, and the ancients were persecuted for what they believed, but slowly, they are returning as we re- gain our connection to our mother, and we start acknowledging and working with the sacred sights once more. By admiring the ancient trees, the variety of unique animals, the smell of a blooming flower in the spring, we get to connect with God's creation on a deep level. Forget about going to Church, the trees are the true church. In fact, it was the churches that got built on the original sacred tree groves and stone circle sites of the original old world."

Luca took his mind back to the garden centre. He was already well practiced at feeling at one with the natural world, but this heart- centred knowledge the old man was talking about deepened his connection further.

"Number nine is having a divine purpose and then believing in that. Most people now do not know what that is, but once you do, you find a new life force within yourself. I think that everybody when they are a small child knows their destiny, it is what they liked to do most, what filled them with passion and purpose. It is our job to find this once more, perhaps even discover a new purpose. We'll know it is the right thing if our hearts start burning alive with passion.

Finally, number 10, the most important one is belief, love and heart. These forces are what give you your life force. When these forces are weak, degeneration occurs. If these are kept powerful and developed, evolution occurs. These forces run every single thing in every universe. These are the forces of the divine itself! When we start to believe in ourselves and in who we are, it changes everything."

Luca had already discovered much from the old man's teachings; but what was funny was that he actually already knew all this deep down; the old man was only awakening what was already inside of him. All the great teachers throughout history all did the same to their students. They never forced anything upon them, they allowed their students to feel for themselves.

As the afternoon drew to a close, the old man congratulated Luca on following his heart to come to Bali and getting in touch with his true self. He told Luca to try his best to connect to his higher self and to nature as much as possible, and that he would explain the importance at a later date.

"One more thing, Luca, one of the main purposes of life that not many know, is no purpose at all. I'll leave you to think about that one."

Luca set off but turned around when he heard the old man shout something.

"Watch the news tonight, Luca."

"Why," Luca shouted back, confused.

"Just watch it, the air has all of a sudden got extremely thick," he said, a chill in his voice, looking up at the darkening clouds, hearing a few distant rumbles of thunder.

Luca was so confused as to why he was told to watch the news but nodded back and waved the old man goodbye.

"When should I return though?"

"I think you will know when to come back."

Luca thought about the old man's strange behaviour all the way back to the hotel, wondering what on Earth he meant, but was intrigued as to what would be on the news that night.

The main headlines were on at seven that night and there was an English channel on his television. It had started to rain heavily outside with rumbles of thunder and flashes of lightning. He never normally watched the news; the negativity and doom and gloom didn't go well with Luca's positive life outlook, but it was only recently he was questioning why the news was actually always like that.

'I wonder when the day will come when the news reporter comes on and says, today, there is no news!' Luca thought to himself, another flash of lightning outside, rain smashing against the window.

The news came on and the reporter spoke....

"The main headline today; a huge war is on the horizon between America and Russia after the murder of the American president. America suspects that Russia was involved in the murder and the evidence for this being true is increasing. America and England both declare martial law as attacks are due. This is a huge shock for the world as no news of a war was even heard of this afternoon; the news has only just filtered in. It looks like the world may just have to brace itself."

Luca turned off the television, bewildered as to how the old man knew what would be on the news before the news even knew itself.

Luca had submerged himself in a magical world, a world of peace and love where no evil could happen, and now he had just entered the 'real world' again. In Bali he had disconnected himself from that world and properly found himself, and now looking at all the fear and anger in the world, he felt he had taken a step back in his development. He had to return to the old man.

The next morning, Luca headed back to the mountains and found the old man once again meditating at his usual spot by the lake.

"How did you know that something so bad was going to happen in the world?"

"Not bad; nothing is good nor bad, it is your perception that makes it so. I will explain more later, but for now, do not be so quick to judge events because they may not be all that they seem. I felt the change in energies in the world, it is all about feelings and intuition."

"I'm not sure I quite understand, how do you manage to stay so calm and still meditate as usual when the whole world is in tension; my family back home included. They rang me last night to make sure I was okay here; they are not used to me being so far away from home at a time like this."

"I manage to stay so calm because I am the observer. I am not part of the fear and confusion, that is not my vibration. Instead, I look down like an eagle to its prey. I see, but I am not affected."

"How can you not be a little scared of war or of what is going to happen though?"

"Because, I trust in the destiny of the world. I live for the present and I do not fear. These three things are why I am not scared."

Now Luca was really intrigued.

'The destiny of the world he mentioned before. He talked about how love will rule. He must know the future then,' Luca thought.

Luca asked him, but he said no. He said that he just felt things in the moment.

"The destiny of the world, Luca, is the destiny that God intended for us. Humanity is starting to see the love once more with the help of the moon, planets, stars, sun, and even the Earth herself. This time has been prophesied by many indigenous cultures. It is one massive collective awakening for humanity. The energies are here, we just need to open our hearts and souls as humanity to them.

Some civilisations predicted this awakening thousands of years ago! They read the planets and innerstood destiny and nature herself. They were so much more advanced than we are now even though so many people think we are the cleverest race. I tell you something, we are currently the thickest race ever! Degrees and intellect mean nothing, Luca. Look at a bee and a flower; they work together in a symbiotic relationship, a natural intelligence. They already have all the answers. We are part of that, yet we forget we are, so we seek answers from the new brain and from somebody else who apparently has what you call a 'degree.' A flower does not think to itself, 'I need others to tell me how to live, how to act or how to be in health,' it just knows. It just lives. The flower cannot be a better flower. It is perfect as it is because it knows itself. It is in a state of 'being,' and being its authentic self as an individual expression of the collective. Just like a flower, we need to simply 'be'. We aren't called human BE-ings for no reason.

We do not need to search outside of us or to act a certain way to fit in. We need only to live with freedom, and to connect with our hearts like nature does. We need to know ourselves as much as the flower knows itself. Authenticity is the highest possible vibration."

"Wow," Luca shouted, "You have just explained modern society so well. That is why people are so depressed, ill and feel worthless. They are trying to be something they are not, and they are not being authentic to themselves and true to their hearts. They are not living their truths so they are living a lie."

"Exactly Luca, and this leaves the soul extremely wounded."

"Everybody needs to find their purpose, their destiny," the old man continued. "They need to find how they can be of service to the world in a way that lights up their being and brings joy to the heart. To work is your service and to play is your purpose; both are intertwined. By service and work, I simply mean what you are passionate about to contribute towards a balanced world and a balanced humanity. My work for example Luca could be teaching you and teaching the truth. That would be my service, or one of my services at least. The majority of people are doing a meaningless job; by doing that they are doing a disservice to their souls."

Luca nodded in agreement. The old man could see in Luca's eyes that he innerstood.

"Thousands of years ago, a group of people consumed by fear have been trying to control the world. They are frightened that if people awaken, they will lose all their authority and power, so they have been controlling the media, governments, health, education, money and the entire system to keep people bowing down in compliance. Keeping people in fear and anger and fighting against each other is their game. It is the only way they can control a population. If humanity was in a state of love and authenticity, we would be uncontrollable, wild and free. The only way out IS to be authentically you! Now, with the murder of the president and the 'war', it is a final desperate attempt to keep people in fear and divided. Fear and division equal manipulation. It is easy to give up your rights when in fear. If they fail with this plan though, that is it, game over. If they succeed, it is total enslavement for humanity. They will always try to keep humanity in fear. Black vs white. Jew vs Christian, one party versus another, what rubbish! This keeps us from figuring out where the real problem lies. They desire total control. They can only be victorious though if as a collective, humanity continues to sleep. If enough people awaken to who they truly are during this time, we could end up with a true heaven on Earth!! Luca, this war has been staged. They are all actors; this is why in governments they call them 'acts' when they 'force' fake laws upon the population!

Distractions are everywhere Luca; in the news, in society and in spirituality itself. A lot of the information in so- called spirituality is pulling us out of our hearts and authenticity, pulling us out of the divine plan and nature, and eradicating us from the main purpose of life: fun. We need to go back to basics and remember how the child lives before conditioning of education, family and society injure their spirits. We were all children once, smiling, laughing, playing, dancing, observing and learning. Children see everything how it is, how it REALLY is. They sense and feel the magic that binds all things; seeing the beauty that is all around them, even in something so simple as a leaf, they see awe and wonder. Most of all though, they are a living embodiment of what God intended for us humans to be, love, magic and wonder. What a life it really is to be experiencing creation!!!"

Luca was captivated by the old man's energy and words. He resonated with all he said. He was beginning to innerstand that the spirit of every individual gets targeted by education, lies and 'real life' until they lose their essence, their purity, becoming a slave to the system and a shadow of who they once were. Luca seemed to be one of those individuals who had an immunity to the lies. He felt the truth in his being, to ancient wisdom. The journey he was on in Bali was only awakening what was dormant inside of him; truth that is dormant inside us all, albeit more so in others, but it is still surely present.

Luca though still had many questions for the old man. 'Who were the controllers? What is their aim? Why are they so evil?' But most of all, 'how do we eradicate them from our world?'

"Before I got onto telling you about the bigger picture, I just want to say that even the controllers themselves can re- balance. Yes, we need to call what they have done out, but then we must also work towards hoping that one day, they too will find the compassion and love they once held before they lost their ways completely. It is all part of the evolution of humanity, because at some level humans themselves have chosen to walk this path."

Luca was trying to innerstand the depths of the old man's words.

"Ok Luca, I am going to tell you a story; not many innerstand the bigger picture and the reality of what we are dealing with. Some believe it is just about money and power. Some believe they are trying to attach humans to an artificial reality to control us totally. Some think they are trying to wipe out the majority of humans and enslave the rest. In a sense, all have some truth, however even though both have their truths, none are THE truth. There are many theories going around, but what we need to do is see things from a higher perspective. Too many get caught up in a concept and cannot develop further from it, they become stagnant. The higher perspective is where most people who think they are awakening don't get to. There is always a larger picture at play. How do we know where we are going if we don't know where we have come from in the first place? Now, let me take you back in time into our true history.

"A long time ago, a great empire was built. Not an empire with oil, money, business and low life nonsense, but an empire of peace, justice, unity. An empire where nature was respected and honoured. They innerstood that we belong to the Earth. Our Earth is our mother Luca."

Luca was all ears for the old man's story, taking in each and every word of wisdom.

"The empire was built upon values. Values that protected and nurtured nature, working with it and not against it. Values that included every man, woman and child as equals, each giving a unique service. A world of peace and beauty and of co-operation. The people of this time knew of the interconnectedness between all things; they knew that the people, the plants, the animals, the stars, sun and moon and even the landforms were all part of the one. This all came from the aboriginals, the people that were and still are the most connected to the natural world. They knew that everything has spirit, a unique spirit, but that we are all a part of one huge, interconnected soul. They innerstood that humans are not above nature, and that if we ever tried to go above nature, which we try all the time, there would be huge consequences. Everything is energised by spirit, Luca; the rain, the wind, the soil, each has spirit, and works with everything else to create balance. It is important to know though that they also innerstood that there is a visible world and an invisible world. There are infinite worlds co- existing; worlds beyond time itself. These forces and the spirits that live in these worlds can help guide humanity when they feel the need. They called them the spirits of the ancestors. They also knew there were guardians, nature spirits, celestial spirits, and so on... When people use things like internet now, or simply switch on a television with a remote control, do they not then stop to question that if they cannot see the beam travelling from the remote to the television, or the internet and radio waves travelling right in front of their eyes, that there is also a chance that there is so much more going on that we also cannot see; things in other dimensions, spirits, guardians; or a whole other host of other things. There are infinite forms of waves literally everywhere, Luca."

"I have always felt that too; every time I sat out under the stars at night, I just felt how infinite the universe is. The mind can never grasp that concept, so we just have to feel it as best as we can. The stars are the gateway to the infinite."

"Exactly Luca! What you feel is the truth. When we look at the stars, we feel humbled, and I really love that feeling.

There is magic everywhere shaping every life, so many do not even take notice of it. Some first become aware of these forces through synchronicity, through numbers, through unexplained events, and so on. The magic goes way beyond these things though. I like to call this magic, the 'high magic.' This is the force of the divine. It is the force that blows the winds, that makes synchronicities happen, that grows the plants. It runs through moments, interactions, deeds and actions. Once we become aware of this force, we take our power back. We then become part of the dance of creation. Instead of dancing way off the rhythm, we become the rhythm, we become the co- creator. I know you feel this, Luca, you were aware of it by coming to Bali and meeting me. You have become a driver of your own destiny."

Luca simply smiled. Now he was aware of what it truly was, he had a new appreciation for the guidance he had to come to Bali and meet with the old man. He too saw this force everywhere he looked, feeling it flowing in his blood.

"I will continue now explaining the bigger picture." The old man said.

"Back then the Law itself was known to all. The foundations of life were put in place, and the Law was placed so that the world was kept in balance. It ensured that every human knew of their connection to the natural world and their responsibilities to maintain the balance of the world. The law ensured that everybody knew of their connection and duty towards other people, other aspects of life, the land and the spirits in other dimensions. That law still stands now, but it has been forgotten. The Law they are using now with this martial law is not law at all! It is dictatorship or admiralty law; they make you believe it is law when it is not! The fake law the controllers use is all about consent; if you do not consent to their system, the law does not apply to a living man who stands under natural law or the law of God only.

The rest of the 'law' is made only to enslave the population into thinking they are free, when really they belong to a tyrannous system. It is clever how they manage to make people give consent, but it works, unless you know the true law.

So much greed and power came into the world before the great empire of freedom and peace was created. The values that humans should live by were desegrated just as they are now in our recent times. When greed and power take over, the connection to nature is lost, and therefore we get lost! The world was in disarray, total disconnection to what life was about and to nature. How this greed and power overtook the peace and beauty is still a mystery; it was likely, like I said, that humans got too technologically advanced, too consumed by greedy desires and became too 'powerful' in more than one way. The connection to the foundations of life were lost. The greedy ones saw that humans could be manipulated. They saw that they could play God, or at least they thought they could. Like in the legends of Atlantis, they say the God's themselves destroyed the kingdom of Atlantis because most of the people got too greedy. I really believe this was the case in real life until peace returned, and the values also returned. Atlantis was a real event that occurred, and that we must learn from now to stop anything like that happening again. We must look at ourselves in the mirror and ask ourselves, what truly matters?

The man that united the world from the tyranny and greed once more, and who ran the greatest empire ever, Luca; an empire of peace, oneness; and an empire that respected and nurtured the land, was the greatest king this world had ever known. The king back then innerstood the importance of staying balanced. He knew that status was of no importance; but the people respected and honoured him in respect of that. He also respected and honoured the people in return. There was harmony between the king and the people. He destroyed the greed and brought about the age of peace. He was a living embodiment of truth. He innerstood the magic that binds the Earth, and had the innate feeling of internal magic, a love for existence. He was the man who brought about delivering the message from the creator that life really is about them four things I mentioned to you not long ago; fulfilling your own soul desires, helping nature and humanity thrive out of a pure heart, achieving your own destiny, and to better yourself in some way every day. He knew the importance of fun, honesty, respect, and authenticity. He was the greatest leader, as he was no leader. He desired no power, no authority, although all respected him. He followed natural principles and grounded them to the Earth. His name was King Arthur, destined to bring about the age of Albion; and his wife was Queen Guinevere who was just as important to the world. There were many individuals that helped Arthur create that world, and they were all honest, honourable people who shared the same vision. Arthur wouldn't have been able to do it on his own, he had good people by his side of no less importance than himself. He innerstood the importance of working together to achieve freedom in the world. He truly innerstood the way nature worked, and he looked at nature as an example as to how humans should live; in balance and in co-operation with each other. What a fantastic world he created.

King Arthur's kingdom somehow was defeated, although the strength and power of the truth that Arthur lived by at that time will live forever. It is what the world is made from; what binds everything in existence. The kingdom will return but there will be challenges. There are beings in the universe so lost that they have lost the connection to God, the love, and so seek to manipulate the world instead. If all humans are connected to their hearts and innerstand 'truth,' by listening to what feels right, manipulation and control cannot succeed! Whoever wants to conquer natural law will never be victorious; it may look like it temporarily, but in the long run, no chance, the laws of nature will hold strong. The ones that have been controlling humanity for such a long time know that this time NOW is the great awakening, so they are doing absolutely everything to keep their power; but we as a human race are waking up so fast! They will be powerless once we reach a level of community, a level of love and a level of innate connection to ourselves and nature once more."

Luca was feeling blessed to be learning so much about life only a short while after he was longing to find answers. He had manifested his reality because he was pure of heart.

"Why are the controllers like this though; how did they become so evil and want to destroy the peace?"

"Power and greed corrupts, Luca, along with the reality that through subtle conditioning and pulling people away from nature, it was possible to control this realm. This thought got all consuming for them. However, all is not lost, even for them. They have like I have said before, simply lost who they are. It is always possible to find yourself again.

"Arthur was not just any king Luca. He was the once and future king," the old man said, looking at Luca with a deep smile, his eyes piercing Luca's soul, teaching him the purest of truth. Arthur is destined to bring about the age of Albion in this realm's time of need. And that time is now."

Luca was mesmerized by the old man's words, feeling now part of something much bigger than he would ever have thought possible. He never realised the severity and the scale of deception playing out in our world. Now it was making sense why people were so lost as he walked the streets back home.

"Arthur is destined to rise again in Albion's time of need. Whether he has already risen or about to rise is for us to discover Luca, but all we know is the disconnection from ourselves and great spirit is at an all-time low. To bring about this age we need to remember who we are; infinite spiritual beings living temporary human experiences to the best level we can possibly achieve, feeling the most alive we can. To awaken the masses, we have to be the best, most authentic version of ourselves, giving out love to the masses and all of nature. Every good morning to a stranger counts. To help others, we must first help ourselves. We need to evolve every single day, spiritually, emotionally and physically to become better human beings which in turn affects everybody else to better themselves. The energetic shift is happening and can only happen if we are aligned with the natural truth of who and what we are. The ancestors, God, and even the Earth itself is watching over every one of us at this magical time to be alive."

Luca was in awe of the old man. He was old yet he swam, walked and had ten times more energy than most twenty-year-olds seemed to have that he saw. He was living proof of what he taught.

"Too many people preach something, but do not actually live it. How can you trust somebody that does not live their truth?" Luca thought, inspired by his teacher.

Luca was staring into the old man's sky-blue eyes, engrossed. His eyes looked like they had seen much. They had captured so much wisdom and ancient teachings during their time here. His eyes seemed to hold the key to the entirety of existence through their sparkle.

"I will leave you alone now by the lake, Luca, I have taught you much and I think that you need some time alone with your thoughts."

Luca sat by the lake for hours, and the sun was just beginning to set beyond the mountains. The air began to get a little chillier, but still Luca sat, contemplating all what he had been told. He was beginning to see the world and the deceptions for what they really were.

The old man returned once the first stars started to appear in the sky above. The full super moon was now out, and as big and bright as Luca had ever seen it, its light shimmering in the lake below.

"How are you feeling Luca?"

"I have never felt better in my entire life; I am starting to innerstand who we are as humans and why they have been controlling us the way that they have been. If we innerstand that we are a free soul living a human experience as a FREE being, what have they to control? You have taught me so much; I am eternally grateful!"

"It's not even just about them, Luca. Also, what have we to control. So many people rationalize and want control over every event in their lives. They do this out of fear. Once we trust and surrender, we lose the sense of having to have total control over everything. There is a difference between being the creator of your life and having total control in a fearful way. For example, if we want to find an aligned relationship, we don't just go to a bar and try to get with anybody, no, we surrender that just by living our truth and talking to whoever feels right, we will find our soulmate.

There is still another important aspect to this that I want to tell you about now.

Luca once again turned his body to face the old man.

"So, as you know, modern society in particular sucks the life force from the people. Remember, the controllers want people as angry, as fearful and as depressed as possible. They want them unwell and sad enough that they are just about kept alive to keep society running. Strong enough to feed the system, but weak enough so that they don't realise their true power as humans. There are many individuals, you included Luca, who already sensed without being told that this is not how life is meant to be lived."

Luca gazed at the stars above, now shining brighter, the moon also, feeling grateful for the innate knowledge that he had.

"Life is meant to be lived with purity, passion; a desire to live and not merely exist. It is to be kept simple, because when you keep it simple, you get life! A love for life is why we are here, it's that simple."

"You are right," Luca replied, resonating. It was only the other day when I was admiring a tree that had fallen almost to the ground, hanging on to life; however new growth and new flowers were growing out of the old fallen trunk. It was that desire to live that allowed the tree to keep living. The tree just loved life and did not want to move on yet. It was evolving and adapting to the situation," Luca said, almost as wise as the old man himself.

The wise old man was overjoyed hearing the young man's experience and clever observations. He knew that Luca was indeed a wiseman himself, and the old man knew something about Luca that he didn't even know himself. He didn't need to know just yet. He was on a journey, and the divine plan was flowing perfectly for him.

"Yes Luca, the old man continued, the love for life is the law of existence. Without this law, nothing works. A lot of seemingly wisemen have forgot this, going to deep and losing their paths. Remember, the point of life is no point at all; it is purely to live, to enjoy, to experience this realm with our senses, our natural attractions. Life is pure bliss; it is pure magic. God never created this life to be complex, he created it to be simple so that everybody can access the truth. The truth about life can be written on the palm of your hand."

Luca's heart was expanding beyond all words hearing what the old man was saying. He thought to himself, 'you know something is true when it feels so right and natural in the heart."

"Back to society though; they want to eliminate all excitement, all wonder from life, and therefore the spirit of life itself by creating the illusion of work for a pointless cause, a nine until five, bills, mortgages, boundaries, limits, false worries, destruction of nature, false prophets and gurus; the list goes on. This is not just for western society, but it is the most fitting term to use for the purpose of explaining this. It is the entire world and its collective way of life near enough. The ones outside of this are the awakened ones like you and me, and trust me, Luca, there are many more of us out there, and we will find each other.

All these things destroy the freedom of the inner child that we should live by and build on. The majority are unhappy with their lives and rightly so. They are given an illusion of freedom, be it a new house, a new car, when it is not freedom at all, just another bill to feed the system. Most people anyway pay bills for a house they only use to sleep in to then go to work the next day, and they pay bills for a car they drive to work to earn money to pay for that car! Ridiculous."

Luca was impressed by the old man's passion, reminding him exactly of himself when he was questioning things back home with the house and car analogy.

"We can all half escape from this. We can find a job that we like, we could satisfy some of our passions and we can pretend the system isn't there; but that is not the answer. The system will still be there, the money will still be corrupt and 'authorities' and the 'controllers' will still be in charge of the world. The answer right now is to live life on our own terms as best as we can whilst getting the people together to build a new, fair system. This will take time, I know, but it is essential if we want a fair, free world. This system cannot sustain itself, especially for the awakened individuals who just will not tolerate this anymore. People will find each other and come together to create a new world. The more people awaken to the truth, the more the current system will lose power. So many people are born into this world like yourself Luca who are already awake; this is as a result of the energies in the world; a new humanity is nearing, and the people who are already here are also being pushed to awaken themselves, sometimes by ones that are therefore younger than them."

Luca took his mind back to where it all began, at the conversation between the two old women at the garden centre, and how they were talking about life being about getting a decent job to get by. His journey to the truth began since that day, and here he was, sitting with a true wiseman that innerstood the way that life really worked.

"The controllers certainly have done a good job at keeping people in this state for so long!" Luca exclaimed, looking around at Bali's mountain range, amazed that beyond the simple beauty of the mountains was that illusionary society.

"Yes, but the time has come for it to end. This is why the controllers are doing everything in their power now, and with this 'war,' it is their final shot when it comes to keeping people enslaved. It could go two ways Luca; one being total tyranny and total loss of freedom and spirit; and two being the journey to total freedom and regaining our spirit. Only WE decide the outcome. We heal the world by healing ourselves, and by giving thanks to the Earth and skies for this blessing of a life."

It was getting late; Luca thanked the wiseman for his teachings, explaining that they had touched his heart and changed him forever, and then headed back to the hotel on the back of the old man's motorcycle.

Luca chuckled to himself at the sight of the old man whizzing around on a motorbike, his energy never fading. His way of life kept him young.

He felt utterly invigorated by Bali's beauty and the days lessons.

In bed that night, Luca took his mind back to the short time he had been in Bali so far. He pondered over the lessons he had learnt and the truth that he had found within himself, speechless at all the synchronicities that led him to even be in Bali in the first place, and then the continuing synchronicities once he had arrived. It was truly a remarkable feeling. He was being guided and looked over, and an overwhelming feeling over gratitude came over him, creating an urge in his heart to give something back to the land and spirits of Bali in thanks for the synchronistic journey he had been on.

In the morning, at sunrise, Luca got up and found a stone that had an energy that stood out to him and threw it in a nearby stream as an offering. Getting emotional, he lay at the bank of the stream, listening to the tranquillity of the running water with huge ferns next to him swaying gently, almost as if they were trying to communicate with him. In reality they were; every living being on Earth is constantly communicating with each other in a language beyond words that humans need to re-gain contact with just like Luca had. It was a language of pure love. The universal language.

The Earth loves offerings; it shows you care and that you love Mother Earth, and that you know that you are one with her and are grateful to have the chance to walk on her lands. We should class ourselves privileged to get the chance to live in this incredible realm, just like Luca.

Soon Luca will innerstand the most important teaching yet, but first he will be tested in ways that will test his will, his strength, and most of all; his heart.

3

chapter

The clouds started to gather above the mountains that Luca was scrambling down, his legs starting to ache after a long day's hike. He had just managed one of his hardest hikes yet, six hours of walking that he began at sunrise. It was now mid-afternoon, and he was finally returning to ground level where he left off.

He saw a small entrance to a cave to his left; it was just tucked away enough that most people would miss it, but not Luca, he was always alert and observing things. He took a glance inside.

"What do you think you are doing!" a voice shouted, echoing inside the cave.

"I, I, am just."

Luca couldn't get his words out, too shocked that there was anybody inside.

"I was in the middle of a meditation, and you just interrupted me."

"Well how was I supposed to know that anybody was in here?" Luca snapped back.

"Have you no senses, no instincts. Could you not feel that there was any presence inside?"

In all honesty, Luca did not develop any feelings that there was anybody nearby. He was too preoccupied with the views and his curiosity.

Already Luca was doubting himself, even from this little confrontation; and although it may not seem like it yet, the psychological battle for Luca's mind had begun.

"Come in young man, I am sorry I shouted at you, would you like a cup of nettle tea?"

"Emm, yeah why not," Luca replied, relatively cautious to the man's offering but happy that the man apologized to him.

Luca adjusted his eyesight to the cave. It wasn't completely dark as there was still daylight filtering through, but he still had to strain a little to make out a clear view of the man who's cave he was now sipping tea inside.

The man looked roughly sixty; thin, pale, and quite short. He didn't look like he ventured outside to often. He had a few small wrinkles and came across as a very serious man on a dedicated mission which was currently unknown to Luca. He didn't look local, in fact he looked quite English.

"What is your name?" the man asked.

"Luca, and yours?"

"Samnal," the man replied.

"It is nice meeting you Luca; what brings you to Bali anyway, most people your age who come here travel with somebody else, but you are alone I see."

"I came in search of answers to existence."

"Go on, explain." Samnal said, curious.

"I always have had strong, connected feelings to life, God, and the universe, and not so long ago I was working back home and overheard a conversation between two older women talking about how life is about plodding through with a decent job just to get by comfortably. I came here as I knew that just couldn't be the way life is meant to be, there had to be more to it, so I followed my heart and the omens which led me here."

Luca briefly told Samnal about the old man and his dream before he came, so now Samnal had a clearer picture as to why Luca was so far away from home, spending who knows long in a foreign land.

"Luca, what you tell me about your experiences here in Bali, and the synchronicities you had leading up to coming here are very interesting. It seems as if you really are an awakening individual that simply needs a help in hand in finding the correct path. I think I can help you with some very important teachings, that in my experience teaching others, will lead you to where you need to go."

Luca was listening, feeling slightly uneasy, after all, he was not used to spending so long in the darkness of a cave.

"There is only one path to the truth young man. You must follow the path of pure discipline and sacrifice. This is the only path to really get to the true enlightenment. Do you understand Luca?"

Luca didn't nod, but merely carried on staring at Samnal. His entire being felt uneasy and on edge about what he was preaching.

"What do you mean exactly?" Luca said, hoping that he would explain.

"Well, to get to the truth we firstly need discipline. Discipline meaning to keep to a path or a schedule. For example, I sit here in this cave and meditate up to four hours a day in darkness. I am teaching myself discipline. I sacrifice the pleasures of everyday life to keep on at my journey to the truth. I don't want to waste time doing pointless things when I could be working hard! The one who works the hardest, eliminating the taunts of life's pleasures will be victorious in reaching the truth.

Secondly, we need to know that this life is just to prepare us for reaching illumination in the next life, or awakening shall I say. We can do this by using so many different practices, but it is vital to keep to the disciplines and place them as the most important thing you need to be doing everyday above all other things, especially enjoyment or whatever other useless passions you have, they are like taunts from the devil they are. Like really, what are people trying to achieve by playing and smiling and laughing on the beach, what are they work-ing towards? I see so many people come to Bali wanting to have the time of their lives on the beach, partying and laughing all night long. Good luck to them, but they for certain will not find enlightenment in this life! I once fell for it nearly when I was younger, but I met a teacher myself who showed me the right way and I have stuck to it since. I think that you, young man are in a similar situation as I was when I was your age, and I really think I can help you.

Thirdly, suffering is also absolutely vital when it comes to the awakening process, it makes us harder, and it develops our souls for the next life. This life is made to be full of suffering so that we no longer have to suffer in the next life because we already then have en-lightenment due to our hard work in this life. All the suffering is for a reason. We have to put these things as priorities. If you want to be like the others then so be it, but if you want to truly find the truth and awaken yourself, Luca, you must listen to me."

"But the teacher that I just met said completely the opposite to all this!"

"Well, he thinks he has reached the truth and enlightenment, but he has not, he wouldn't be on this Earth if he had, he would be in heaven or in some sort of higher dimension."

Luca had no reply to this, he was starting to believe that Samnal might be right about some of this.

"I have always valued discipline, Samnal, but I always thought it to be a positive thing to get you to achieve your goals in this life. Disci-pline is not suffering; it's just about being focused on your goals and making it a daily practice to reach them. Like with gym, you push through the pain to get stronger, but it's not a bad pain, just a little uncomfortable. I agree we must push ourselves out of our comfort zone, but what you're saying just doesn't feel right. It seems so nega-tive. Your entire life revolves around suffering."

"Yes, my entire life does evolve around it, discipline and suffering must come before all else! I have followed all the best teachers before me. They set the path out for others to follow; that means I must be on the right path if I am following all the ones that said they had reached enlightenment through this way. You must follow the ones who have already done this and have led the way. They are showing us the one and only path to true enlightenment. You now have a chance to do this. You have met me for a reason young man."

"And they all followed the path of suffering and sacrificed the happiness that life gives?" Luca asked, getting worked up.

"Of course, they had no time for little things that gave them a bit of happiness that they would then forget about the next day, they wanted to find the truth that would last with them and take with them into eternity."

"But it wouldn't fade. People always remember the happiness that they experience, they don't just forget about it the next day, it lasts a lifetime."

"Oh, you always have some kind of answer don't you boy, you either listen to me or get out my cave and leave me to find the truth."

"Can I not ask questions? I don't just take what somebody says as the final answer."

"I have told you, I am following the one and only way to enlightenment, there are no questions to be asked, you either follow or get left behind. Did you not go to school, the teachers hate it when you ask questions of them."

"I did go actually, and I always felt what they taught was wrong, that life is not how we have been told; that is the reason why I came here, to find the truth. I never agreed with teachers at all at school, they have been conditioned to teach the same old crap as the ones before them were taught!" Luca said, now getting a little angry.

"Well, I'm giving the truth to you. The people who I follow are true teachers, people who have found the truth of all. Feelings, what is that all about! They are just a distraction again, look boy you either listen or you don't, I am offering you my help and it is the most important decision of your life if you take it or not; not many people get the opportunity to find the truth!"

"But Samnal, what do you hope to get out of all this; I know you said enlightenment, but what is enlightenment for you exactly? In the next world once you have this 'enlightenment' what do you imagine yourself feeling?"

"I don't know exactly how I will feel; I'm not sure feeling even comes into this, you have an obsession with feeling, sometimes you must sacrifice feelings!" His voice was raising slightly, and he was beginning to get agitated with the boy who was questioning his methods. "There is one path put out for us all, and that is the path we must all find, everything else is wrong. What you seem to have been taught by that old man is an easy, soft, too good to be true way to enlightenment. It can never be that simple Luca. If it was that easy everybody would achieve it."

"Everybody can achieve it though, it's within all of us!" Luca said, questioning what he believed now Samnal had poisoned him with his words; doubts were creeping in fast.

"I'm only saying what the ones before me have said, and what I firmly stick to, I know this is the way."

Luca didn't know how to deal with the man who had a completely different outlook on life and awakening. 'I resonated so much with the old man, but maybe this man is right about the old man, he wouldn't be on Earth if he had already achieved a full awakening. Samnal seems so certain in his ways. I know the old man did too, but what if Samnal is right, I would have to change the way I go about things in life to achieve a full awakening.'

Luca's spirit felt depleted, damaged, and his energy had been sucked. It was like somebody had just told him of some terrible news. His entire beliefs of life being about passion, desire, heart, peace, enjoyment, experience and a connection to nature, and of course a balance of discipline and hard work were being told they were an unnecessary distraction and a diversion from the 'truth'. The reason for this; a man in a cave who practices sacrifice and discipline as the only important things in life, day in and day out.

Luca thought to himself, 'A man who has this much experience in life practising this everyday must know a lot more than me, a young man only just starting to discover things and learn about life.'

"So, Luca, think about this, and come and see me again tomorrow if you want and I can take you through some of the basic things I first learnt of."

Luca managed a smirk, walking away after reluctantly thanking Samnal for his hospitality. He felt deflated, absent of energy, and the way he saw life itself had been damaged. Everything seemed different; it seemed darker, and the magic had vanished, even though the birds were still singing exactly the same in the trees above.

'There must be some truth in what Samnal was preaching,' he thought, his mind all over the place, his peace of mind diminished. All the experiences and memories with Bali and the old man replaced with fears and doubts. It was as if his own life force was being sucked away from him right in front of his eyes.

The old man was needed; Luca needed to see him!

The next morning, after a terrible night's sleep with a mind full of doubts, he went to seek out the old man in the mountains.

He was not in his usual spot by the lake, so he wandered into the village, getting more and more anxious to find him.

He had to meet with him. He reinforced all the beliefs he had ever felt and thought about life, and therefore needed him to explain exactly why Samnal was preaching something entirely different.

The villagers were playing cards when Luca entered, searching his eyes desperately to find the old man. He could not see him.

"Excuse me," Luca said to a middle-aged man, gently as to not disturb their card game.

"Yes."

"Have you seen," .... Luca paused. He didn't even know the name of the old man he was after.

"Emmm, an older man, large beard; the man who likes to sit by the lake up in the mountains?"

Luca hoped so much that he was around; he needed answers.

"The man you speak of has not been alive for over 1500 years on this Earth plane, although he has always been remembered here in Bali as the man with all the teachings, and yes, he will be remembered generation after generation as the man who loved to sit and meditate by the lake, next to the tallest peak, always to then take a dip, whatever the conditions."

Luca was lost for words, as anybody would be. The man who came in his dream and gave him all the teachings had apparently been dead for 1500 years!

He sat by the stream running alongside the village, not knowing what to think or do. 'Who is he then? Am I dreaming still? If he is real, why is he speaking to me? All those questions were pounding Luca's young head. He had to take a walk and re- gather his mind.

As he was walking through the woodland on the way back to the hotel, he couldn't help but stop and stare at the beauty of the flowers and listen to the swaying of the trees. It was as if they were whispering the answers of life to him, but he was still so damaged by Samnal's words that he couldn't quite interpret the answers. He used to be able to, before Samnal; but it seemed his connection to source and to life had faded. His head was down, he felt weak. 'If that is the case, if that is how life is meant to be lived, then it's all just pointless!' Luca thought, angry with all he had heard. He was only angry as he was letting it into his reality though, he was opening up to the possibility that what Samnal was saying was true, he was forgetting what he knew to be right in his own heart, and that leaves the heart very hurt, the body and mind feeling weak as a result.

He spotted about forty meters away from him, a group of young children playing at the side of the woods, their parents smiling and letting them have their fun. Luca couldn't help but smile too. The thing about children is that they are unconditioned, unindoctrinated and free to roam their surroundings without many beliefs forced on to them. They simply live out their feelings and their hearts. All they want is to smile, to play and to experience this realm, being loved and loving back. Luca saw this as clear as day, and it re- awoke the feelings of truth that he had always felt that had merely been conditioned out of him by somebody else's beliefs. Luca's smile grew as he re- gained belief, and he found himself thinking of the old man. 'Who is he!' Luca thought back on his teachings, how they resonated in his soul and heart, and how like a child they were, simple, not complex. "The child holds the truth!" Luca shouted, his heart once again coming alive, energy returning to his body.

Luca felt his power, his essence return to him. He realised that what Samnal was preaching may work for him, but not for all. It may not even work for him. 'He might simply be suffering needlessly himself!' He thought. 'It is rubbish what he said about suffering, what is the point of the soul coming down here to live as a human if suffering is inevitable!'

The true meaning of hard work is to give your all to a cause that aligns with your being, or to push through a difficult situation that you find yourself in for growth; it for certain does not mean extended suffering as Samnal was preaching.

He knew deep down that there was a difference between suffering and challenges. Challenges are something that you can overcome and truly develop from, they are temporary so you can then see them for what they were once you have overcome them. Suffering is a continuous cycle of feeling stuck and horrible that is needless once you discover how life really works. Yes there are hard times in life, perhaps even temporary suffering, as of course we have to feel things when they happen, but then we must start anew. Our perception changes when we see something as a challenge to develop ourselves and evolve, or to simply experience the duality of life. The body and soul always strive for balance, not to suffer. This was clear when

Luca's body felt re- energized once he re-claimed his power and core beliefs.

Luca thought, 'If Samnal took a moment to speak to his three-year-old self, I do not think he would be wanting to live that way, and he certainly wouldn't push a belief onto a young man.'

Feeling pitiful now for Samnal, he wondered just how many life experiences he was missing out on.

As Luca was about to leave the site of the children playing with a fresh, new spring in his step, as he had now developed from a test of character and belief, he heard a rustling from behind. He turned around to see. It was the old man!

"Oh my God, it is you!" Luca blurted, not believing his eyes.

"I know wise Luca, you have many questions for me, however I do not think you have questions about life anymore, do you? I think you solved them five minutes ago. I saw you with the children, you saw the truth in their playing. I think your questions now are about me, who I am and where did I go."

Luca stared at him for a while, still shocked that he was once again talking to the old man straight after he regained his power, who had apparently passed away over 1500 years ago. 'How did he know that I was questioning life? He must have seen me looking deflated and then smile after I saw them kids playing!'

"Number one question before we start; what is your name!" Luca said with humour, both of them laughing.

"I have many names, and I have been called many things over the years, but you Luca, shall call me brother, because after all, us humans are all brothers and sisters."

Luca was satisfied with his answer, feeling at peace this time with the company he was in.

"So, brother, tell me about yourself, who are you, why are you helping me, are you alive or dead!"

"All fantastic questions brother, Luca, and I shall answer all of them; let's sit and talk over there by the waterfall."

They both took a seat on the rocks by the waterfall, it's natural power and presence making itself known.

"The spirits of the water," the old man said almost to himself. "Water is a magical force, everything in life is water. It is no coincidence that everybody wants to be around water, be it play in it, bathe in it, listen to its music, and of course drink it. It is the essence of existence, as I mentioned to you before. Of course, it comes along with fire, Earth, air and great spirit. Great spirit binds all the elements together, it is the magic that allows life to flow, and it has been called many names over time, similar to me."

Luca was happy to be drinking in his words once again, the roaring of the waterfall next to them.

"Ok Luca, the first thing you need to remember is that nothing dies. This physical reality is just an experience in a solid body. This body expresses our soul in this lifetime until our soul is ready to explore and experience somewhere else. Whilst we are in this body, we need to stay firmly grounded to it, connected to it, and listen to our bodies at all times. Our bodies are the connection we have to the present moment, and that is what this life is all about."

"Just knowing that you are an eternal being living a temporary human experience with unlimited potential and freedom just brings new life force to you," Luca replied back to the old man, enthusiastically.

"But Luca, something that many forget that is very important is that you are not going to be around forever as a human! Just as you were somewhere else before you came here, you will go somewhere else after, consciously, if you pass the game of life by fulfilling the purposes. This means that you must make the most of each and every day, living every experience and goal you have ever wanted. So many take life for granted, when at any moment it could all end. Every breath is precious."

These words of truth gave a new power to Luca; a feeling of powerful life force, will and determination to live to the fullest. The old man certainly knew what he was doing when he was teaching. He felt alive, truly alive when he was in the presence of truth; a tingle all over his body; a pulsating energy flowing through his being, resonating with his heart. Luca thought back to Samnal. 'What the old man says feels so much better than what that idiot was preaching, I feel sorry for the guy!'

"Luca, whatever makes you feel alive and free is the truth. Whatever makes you feel trapped, confused and uneasy is an outright lie."

This was the most important quote Luca would ever live by.

"What about you brother, how are you in a physical body now, who actually are you, why is it me you are teaching these lessons to?"

"I have the ability to incarnate at will into any form I see fit. To help you, I have chosen to come back into my body, as I was in all those years ago. You Luca have also incarnated now at will, although you have forgotten, which is completely natural for a human to do. This is because the human can then learn a lot more about who they really are. The only difference right now between me and you is that I can remember that I have incarnated into this body. You have been born a physical human for a reason; this is your destiny."

"But why are you guiding me of all people?"

"Luca, I am your designated guardian for your journey on Earth. I chose you to guide as you are pure of heart. You have no agendas, and you are destined to bring about the true age of peace and freedom on Earth. The age where every soul can experience life to the fullest, where every tree and living thing is respected and honoured as the sacred thing it is. I know you have always had strong, loving, connected feelings towards the universe and the creator, and your journey in Bali so far has only strengthened these feelings. I gave you an important test the other day in the form of Samnal. Samnal was me! I needed to test your belief in your own truth, and you passed. It was difficult for you, I know, but it was a much-needed test for your soul and your character. This life is all about tests. Tests of will, of character, and most of all, belief. And remember Luca, so- called 'negative' events always have a deeper meaning, we wouldn't learn and get stronger if we never made mistakes or had lessons to learn."

Luca was utterly baffled, just staring at the old man, a slight smirk on his face signalling his astonishment as to how this man was capable of doing all this.

"So, you really believe in me to help unite this realm?"

"I only believe in you, if you believe in yourself. Do you believe in yourself?"

"Yes, yes I do! I believe in the magic of the Earth around me to help me achieve my vision. I can see a world where we are all truly intoxicated with life and honour this amazing world. There will be no more deceit, no more control, because every human will realise their innate freedom. They will feel the magic that once used to fill their hearts when they were a child."

"Then I believe in you. Come on, Luca, I want to show you something."

They climbed up the side of the waterfall, the rocks glistening in the afternoon rays. They gazed out at the rest of the mountain range from a sort of natural infinity pool, seeing the lake in the distance shining like a crystal.

"Just feel Luca, what all the mystics search so hard to find is right here in the moment. It is in the swaying of the trees, the birds singing, the colours you see. It is in the conversation between you and me, two unique souls. The bliss and true love of life is in these 'small' moments, the present moment. God is here now in these things! People say they cannot see him; have they seen a view like this before? Have they felt a connection? Have they seen, felt and smelt a flower blossoming in the spring? Are they even conscious of their own being, of their senses, of their feelings? Mystics who search outside of this, taking their consciousness out of their feelings in the moment will NEVER find 'God' or 'enlightenment'. Like you experienced with Samnal, they will be constantly searching and never find anything. The truth and God is ALWAYS in plain sight Luca. God is not complex, not something you have to find, and ESPECIALLY not sacrifice your feelings and senses for. We all want to feel. We all want to love, shout, scream, dance, move!!! This is life Luca, come on…. scream!!! Take in the life around us, the magnificent, bewildering, magic creation of the divine creator! The divine is us; we are divine, it's all divine!"

They screamed together at the top of their voices next to the waterfall, life pulsating through their veins.

"I love this realm!" Luca shouted once more.

"Passion is the key," the old man said.

"Just look at the sun, Luca. That sun is giving life to every single thing and every human on this planet. Nothing would live without it. Nothing would live without the trees, the bees, the soil. How people go through life without acknowledging that absolutely every single thing is put PERFECTLY in place so that life can work in balance is beyond me!"

Luca thought about what the old man just said, looking up at the sun, squinting his eyes. 'He is right! Every living thing is so vital for the collective that nothing could live without the other!'

"But that must mean humans themselves are so important to the collective, are we really as important as say, the bee, for keeping this world going?"

"Exactly Luca! Once humanity reaches its destiny, we will discover our true place in the world. We are just as important as anything, there is not one thing on this Earth that is out of place, each has its own unique purpose."

Luca had learnt so much; lessons that would shape him for the rest of his life. He had learnt just the right teachings to take him towards the next stage in his life. He was so grateful for all the old man had taught him, and they had developed quite a friendship. He thanked the old man with all his heart for his wisdom and guidance, explaining that he had changed him forever, allowing him to access his true self. They had made a friendship for life, a soul connection.

A month went by for Luca in Bali and his money saved up from work coming to an end, but he had had the most incredible month inhabiting this new consciousness, this new soul shaking passion for life. The teachings the old man had given him merely magnified what he had always felt inside his soul his entire life so far. It is all about that belief in what you feel.

4

———————

chapter

Luca could hear the crickets as the sun began to set. It had been warm, and a fire gathering was happening on the beach that night. The locals around his age were having a meaningless celebratory barbecue. The best celebrations in life do not have to have a reason. To celebrate something just for the sake of doing it are when the best memories are made.

He flicked off his shoes and lied down, gazing at the dark orange sky, breathing in the sea air. The talking and gentle music in the background made the occasion even more relaxing and enchanting.

The last of the birds made their journeys home for the night. Luca had always loved that, the feeling that everything, even the birds were drawing inwards, resting for the night, and it was left with just him and the first of the stars. He didn't have words to describe the peacefulness, the love and the pure relaxation he was feeling.

Once Luca was left completely by his self though with the dying embers of the fire, he began to wonder what his next chapter would be. Once he had said goodbye to the old man last month, he told Luca to really feel and imagine what his next calling would be. This time, he would receive no signs, he would purely be led by his own feelings.

It was now pitch black and the stars were shimmering brighter than he had ever seen them. Shooting stars flew past, a good omen for Luca, once again making Luca wonder just how much more life is out there than we know about. He then saw strange lights appearing and then vanishing. Perhaps they were drones spying on him bringing out the truth and planning on destroying the controllers. 'No, I prefer to think of them as guardians than spy drones,' Luca thought, smiling.

The stars though helped him to connect to his intuition. They always helped him find that inner peace, and when the mind is at peace, the body and soul are as well, therefore visions and energy can flow. Intuition can be accessed more easily. His next vision was to return home.

Luca got off the plane and arrived in London at the airport. He had never explored London, and with all the buildings and separation from nature, it never really appealed to him. He especially didn't want to after just returning from a heaven on Earth, experiencing things that no human would ever think possible, this day and age anyway.

As soon as he arrived there was talk everywhere of the war that he had seen many months ago on television; the war that led to a very interesting and life changing conversation with the old man.

Talk was everywhere! Televisions, radios, newspapers, posters and banners all around the airport. The energy was so dense, so tense, so negative.

'This is the world that most people live in,' Luca thought, a changed man now that he had returned from Bali.

He had experienced and developed so much that now he was back in what the old man liked to call, the illusionary society, his entire being felt out of place. He knew that this society was created out of lies and deceit. The old man had taught him much. This society kept people in a state of fear, confusion and disconnection.

He observed the people once more, as he did on the streets back home. They were deflated, barely hanging onto life, tired, miserable; he only saw the odd smile, but he tried his best to say hello to everybody, even if they didn't always reply, remembering how the old man emphasised the importance of community, and how the awakening starts simply by saying 'hello' to all.

Luca caught a glimpse of a newspaper, a white, frail man reading it, clearly doing him no good. 'He looks like Samnal!' Luca thought, smirking. 'You cannot be a living embodiment of truth if you look so ill.'

Luca made out the headline of the newspaper, reading: 'Martial law to be declared, all to be in their homes until further notice'.

It looked like 'the war' was taking off. Luca so badly wanted to return to Bali and relax on the beach, but, remembering his visions, he knew he was to be in England.

It was so hard to resist the temptation to just shake everybody and shout the truth in their faces, but Luca knew that was not the answer. You cannot force the truth onto somebody who is not ready.

'If they do not even know themselves and the reality of the universe, how are they meant to innerstand the deceptions? To know yourself is the key. Hardly anybody can tolerate to spend even one minute alone with themselves.'

He was still giving so much love out to the people as that was just who he was, despite his frustrations. It was difficult not to get frustrated though when the people seemed so lost. 'People are falling for the tyranny in pretence of 'public safety!' He thought, wondering how people could be quite so stupid, but trying his best to understand their way of thinking.

Once Luca returned home, his family were overjoyed to see him, having been away for months.

Upon explaining what had happened to his family, they were in a state of bewilderment. They just couldn't grasp that such out of the ordinary events could happen in this life, and especially to their own son!

Luca tried his best to explain the severity of the deception that was playing out in the world; it was difficult for them to innerstand, but with him explaining that a wise old man who had died over 1500 years ago telling him this, they had to take what he was saying seriously. Of course, it was difficult for them to believe, but they knew for certain their son would not lie to them. They knew that perhaps there was a whole world out there beyond their sensory perception.

The entire world was given strict orders to stay at home, eyes fixated on the tell- lie- vision. People were relying on a box in their houses to tell them how to live their lives. Luca was furious. He knew it was all an illusion, but yet he watched helplessly as the entire world suffered, him now included in his own brick prison.

"At least we have a garden," his mother said, half-jokingly.

Luca, unimpressed by her remark replied, "The entire world is my garden! This is not right, it is unlawful!"

He knew that he couldn't just sit by and stay inside his house until some 'authorities' gave an order to be a free again; he would be driven crazy! His freedom couldn't just be taken away.

Days passed though, and the situation grew worse.

Food shortages were announced, water shortages also. It was obvious to Luca that there could never really be a food or water shortage; impossible. Food was everywhere for those with a brain; in the ocean, on the land, in the bushes.... Humans have known how to hunt and gather for a very long time; it was only a food shortage because people were reliant on supermarkets to get their food from.

'Our humanity has been stripped; people have lost their primal survival skills that once allowed us to be self- sufficient. Now people are lazy, weak, and reliant on the system to do everything for them. It's no wonder they are controlled, they are allowing it! They want it!' Luca thought, a little triggered by the lack of aliveness in the people around him. 'The people are slaves; they have neglected all of their god- given human attributes and skills.'

As for the water, the Earth never runs out, like the old man said, it is everywhere. Luca knew for certain that they were making all this up; the controllers that is, to further halt the awakening when it came to humans realising that they are NOT slaves, but free, sovereign beings.

Luca would have no more, he would not stand by and allow them to interfere with his life!

As for the so- called spiritual movement that Luca was seeing all over the internet. That was also a HUGE distraction. Luca innerstood this from his time in Bali where he met Samnal. Samnal was so caught up in escaping life, escaping feelings and escaping his body that he forgot how to live as a human. He forgot who he was. Yes, Samnal turned out to be the old man, but the principle is the same; the old man introduced Samnal to Luca to teach him this very lesson, that now he must keep with him through all the distractions.

The type of spirituality that Samnal was preaching was now all over the internet, distracting all that get caught up in its web. The aim; to pull people as far off their paths as humans as possible. Out of passion, out of purpose and out of nature. They want people monotone, robotic, and bland. 'People are just chasing each other off the hill like sheep.' Luca thought.

Luca concluded that the controllers themselves created the spiritual distraction for the partially awake people that started seeing the lies. They would lead them down the fake spirituality to carry on enslaving humanity.

'The controllers are very well prepared for the eventuality that people will awaken. They need to try everything in their power to stop this awakening. They want no soul, no compassion, no authenticity, even no clear masculine and feminine sides! They detest a fighting for what is right mentality. Nature is their number one enemy. 'Everybody who embarks down the path of finding themselves needs to be extra vigilant!!' Luca thought, shaking his head at all the deception playing out. He was firmly in his power though, and knew that humankind would unite in the end if the belief was kept, just as the old man had said.

He decided that day that he would damn the rules and venture outside on a walk. He was not going to be told how to live his life, no chance. An alpha male, a renegade, a lion not a sheep! Luca remembered what the old man taught him about laws. This was no law! This was tyranny; and Luca did not consent!

On his walk, Luca found himself constantly reminiscing back to his time in Bali, wondering how on Earth he ended up in a situation like this where it was classed as breaking the law if you walked. 'How can I go from Bali to this!' He was concerned for the world, worried for the future, even anxious about the chance of getting caught on his walk.

Suddenly though, whilst watching a couple of buzzards circling in the blue sky above, he remembered the importance of the present moment. The past is history, the future is yet unshaped and a mystery, but the present is a gift. Luca remembered that quote from somewhere, and through that quote he remembered his power. His divine power lies in the NOW, as it does for everybody. Magic can only be created in the present moment.

We as humans constantly get distracted by many different scenarios. We worry about things that we literally make up in our minds; what is nicknamed, 'the monkey brain' and rightly so. These thoughts all come from fears and doubts that stem from a lack of belief and trust in the 'self'. Once you know yourself and your own mind, heart and soul, all of your doubts, fears and insecurities show themselves for what they really are. You can then innerstand where they come from, and work on letting them go.

Luca, despite all the guidance and experiences he had the last year, still had his own doubts and fears. The key is to become aware of them but to not let them control you. Soon enough they will subside, and you will realise most importantly that they were all an illusion in the first place that YOU created!

It was when Luca spotted that an policeman had seen him walking that his fear vanished. He knew his power in the moment and knew how to deal with the law as a living human being. Luca had to step up into his own freedom.

"Excuse me young man. What are you doing out of the house, there is a worldwide emergency. The legislation states that all citizens must abide by these rules."

Luca took a deep breath, and it was as if the old man was inside him.

"I am a living man. No legislation applies to a living man. It only applies to a corporate entity. I do not consent; I do not understand or stand under you. I stand under natural law only. Can you recite your oath please?"

Luca knew that the policeman was shocked. He did not expect that!

He had no choice but to read his oath of conduct which stated all of Luca's freedoms which could never be taken away. It also stated that as a policeman he swore to maintain the true law of the land, or law of God. Do no harm, cause no injury, loss or damage to anybody or their property. The law also stated that it was a severe crime to arrest Luca if he was not committing a crime against natural law.

The policeman became very silent. The truth had shaken the depths of his soul, and he began to feel uneasy as to what he was asking and doing. He knew deep down that it was very wrong.

"I know what I said may surprise you officer, but it is the truth. We have been lied to. You are a human being just like me, and you have no God given right to push unlawful acts against me or the public. Think carefully about what I am saying. Fight for what is right!"

Once the policeman had left Luca to continue his walk, he had two options. One was to protect his pride and his job and carry on pushing unlawful acts; or two, to acknowledge that his entire working life was spent working for a criminal organisation that had no interest in the law or justice, and then educate his colleagues, calling it out. The police work for the people, not the other way around.

The policeman chose the latter and spoke to his colleagues about the situation and the true law. He began to spread the word. This is how the awakening begins; to be fully in your sovereign power, expressing your full self and living your truth. The only way to awaken the world is to BE the world you want to see yourself.

Months went by and the majority of the world was still in fear, still in compliance, but most of the people really believed what they were being told on the news. They were stuck inside watching their little screens while Luca watched the stars.

There did seem to be many waking up to more of the truth, but the distractions of the fake spirituality, false narratives and many other diversions were keeping people from the bigger picture and the authentic truth. Still so many were not in touch with themselves, their own hearts. They were lost on subjects like health, the law, the system. They seemed unhappy, angry, unfulfilled, and Luca could only watch and carry on living his truth. He couldn't change them; he could only nudge them. Working on yourself is the only way. You cannot force change on to another human who is at a completely different stage. Luca learnt this when so many just could not comprehend what he was teaching. Some could, yes, but the majority were not there yet, it just wouldn't register.

As much as he saw hope in the people, he could not stay where he was in England. He had to find a place where freedom and community was still intact, a place where there were more people on his wavelength. He couldn't change the world on his own. He needed help. Of course, there was guidance from the old man, amongst others, but true friendships were what he needed in the moment. He needed to find people with the same pulsating, screaming life force that he had. A people that were just as intoxicated with life. He needed to meet with people with the same vision. He had a vision, and he had a strong feeling in his heart. This could mean only one thing; travel was once again needed. But there was a problem; travel was banned. For Luca though, where there was a problem, there was always a solution.

5

chapter

Luca found out that the high up elite businessmen, or as Luca liked to call them, the controller's puppets, were still being allowed to travel.

'If they can travel, so can I!' Luca screamed, angrily and with determination.

At the airport, Luca was let straight through! No questions asked. Yes, he dressed up in a suit to look rich, but still, was this all propaganda too? Thinking back to the controller's plans and the way they lie about everything; he came to the conclusion that it was.

Arriving in Mexico, he felt so much excitement running through his being, as if great things were about to occur.

He chose Mexico after the place kept coming to him during his times of stillness. Decisions are never difficult when following the heart. The difficult part is listening to the heart in the first place.

Mexico was least affected by the 'laws' and people were still allowed out by the 'controllers' for now. Luca knew that at any moment they could change their minds and the Mexicans too would be confined indoors. He had to make the most of his time.

With his head up, in awe of Mexico, walking along the beach, he spotted a group of people around his age playing volleyball. There were five of them, two young men and three young women, definitely Mexican by the tanned skin tone; although Luca, the sun lover himself was actually not far off.

He stood nearby, gazing out to the oranges of the setting sun, waves crashing to the shore and took in the magnificence of where he was, energy shooting through his being. The energy on the beach where he was that evening was truly beyond words.

Luca straight away had eyes on one of the girls there on the beach playing volleyball, both exchanging glances every so often, maybe even one or two smiles.

The others were glancing occasionally too, perhaps to invite him to play, or perhaps it was the energy that Luca was radiating that night. Maybe it was both.

Luca could see that they had finished their game and were speaking softly to each other.

"Hola, como te llamas," one of the lads said in Spanish, meaning 'Hello, what is your name'.

Luca replied in the best Spanish he could, trying his best to tell them he was English.

"Ahh, you are English, we all know a little English, but Guilia here speaks fluent, don't you Guilia?"

Guilia, the girl that Luca liked, smiled, staring at Luca, "Not completely fluent, but better than all of you."

"You are all speaking perfect to me, better than I can speak Spanish!" Luca said, amused at the fact they thought they couldn't speak yet they were all almost fluent.

They all laughed, Guilia and Luca more nervously than the others.

"So, what are all your names?"

"Okay, so I am Guilia, the other two girls are Francesca and Lucianna, and the boys are Enrique and Jacamo.

Luca smiled, shaking hands with everybody.

They invited him to a game of sunset volleyball, and Luca jumped at the chance, already overjoyed with the people he had met on his first evening in Mexico.

Once they had finished their game, they all sat down together on the beach with some drinks and food.

"So, Luca, how long are you staying in Mexico for?" Enrique asked, his initial thoughts being that Luca was a holiday maker.

"I'm not sure really, it depends."

"Depends on what," Enrique continued, slightly confused.

"It is hard to explain..."

"We have all night," Jacamo interrupted, all of the group eager to know what Luca was doing in Mexico on his own. Guilia was still fixated on Luca, wanting to know herself what he was doing after feeling his positive energy ever since she set eyes on him.

"Ok then," Luca said, smiling at the fact that all of them seemed so eager to find out about his life; still slightly nervous as to how they would judge him after what he was about to tell them.

"So, recently I have returned from Bali in Indonesia. I travelled there in search for answers to life after questioning why society and 'modern life' seemed so wrong last year back at home. I learnt a great deal, and I met a great teacher."

Luca left out the part about the old man being dead for the last 1500 years, not wanting to sound crazy on his first night of meeting them.

"He taught me how life is about experiencing who you truly are and getting to know yourself. He envisions a world where we can learn to live in harmony with the spirit of the world, and our hearts, a community mindset where we are free to live in this amazing world. He explained to me that there is a consciousness he likes to call the controllers that have been manipulating humanity. They have been trying more so than ever to pull us down so that we can never innerstand our true freedom. He said he believes in the divine plan though, and that we must start seeing things from a higher perspective; that it is all for our own benefit.

When I arrived back in England, facing tyranny, I just wouldn't have it; I knew that it was unjust and unlawful, so I finally made a decision to come here to find people like myself where we can go about building the world of peace and unity."

They all smiled at each other, and Luca, not knowing what they were thinking asked, "What are you all smiling at; I know, it is so hard to explain any of this, I understand if you don't know what I am talking about."

He was feeling very anxious at this point, feeling as though he was being judged, especially by Guilia; but realised also that if he was being judged for speaking his truth, they were not the friends for him.

"We are not laughing at you Luca; we know ourselves that what is going on in the world is one huge deception. We are smiling as we are so surprised at the synchronicity here! You think the same as us," Guilia said, mesmerized by the fact that the man she liked felt the same way about life as her.

Guilia, like Luca, had experienced her own unique journey to the truth, and also had strong, connected feelings towards the universe and our true reality from a young age. Everybody's journeys are unique to them, and them alone.

The others were not quite as aware as Guilia at the bigger picture but knew parts of the truth. This was why Guilia was so amazed at the way life worked, bringing somebody into her life at a random time that knew of the same truth she did. Absolutely nothing in life is a coincidence, especially when you're in the flow.

'This life just keeps getting more and more magical,' Guilia thought, knowing that this was just validation that she was on the right path towards her destiny.

"Well Luca, it looks like you have found the group you were looking for, look no further!" Francesca said, feeling the energy of the group herself.

Luca laughed, they all did, taking their time to register the synchronicity of their meeting.

Life works in ways that our rational minds could never hope to innerstand.

"We are grateful that for now things seem fine here in Mexico, but who knows, if they have done that to the rest of the world, who is to say that we are not to join them?" Lucianna said, slightly concerned.

"We have always wanted a sixth member. Like yourself, we all wanted to find people with the same positive outlook on life; somebody that would never say no to a game of sunset volleyball on the beach and then sleep out under the stars. We have also not really known each other for that long, but we all just met and clicked," Enrique explained.

"So, what do you all do in life?" Luca asked.

"Well," Guilia replied, "I currently live in my self- converted van after years of working to save up for the life I dreamed of living. I was travelling around and I met these, right here on this beach!"

"Wow, that is incredible, it's like the ideal life of freedom! You're literally living where your heart takes you, your internal compass. You'll be able to just park up anywhere, watch the sunset each night, and then watch it rise again in the morning, all from the comfort of your van!"

"I know, it has been such a strong dream of mine for so long, and I finally went for it six months ago after it took me three months to convert the van myself. I really loved that term you used, internal compass!"

Whilst Guilia and Luca were both conversing, they both felt a deep connection, like nothing they had ever felt before; as if they had known each other forever. Luca's heart was truly coming alive, and the vision that was planted inside of it as a seed when he was younger was now coming alive with it.

The others lived more local. Enrique and Jacamo were both working with nature on a permaculture project, something that Luca, after years of working in the garden centre had always looked into as something he himself would want to do, actually working alongside nature and healing the world from the destruction of modern horticulture, amongst so much more.

"So can you explain permaculture properly?" Luca asked, wanting to know more.

Permaculture is a practice where plants grow in a system where they are all sharing energy and nutrients with each other instead of grown separately and robotically. It is a communication system where smaller plants, bigger shrubs, waters, soil, and trees all work together as one. The soil is looked after and valued as it is where everything comes from, even us. No artificial products are ever used; it is all done naturally. It shows that the systems of the future for the long game are purely natural. It really does work as well. Systems like this just need more love and care. They need time to flourish. That is something that has been lost in our 'quick fix' and 'patch up' modern life.' Enrique explained, passionate about what he did.

"I completely agree with you, Enrique. People have got their values all muddled up; they think money comes first. When values are lost, we end up with a society like we have. We must re- balance ourselves sooner rather than later! Just working with the land and loving the land is what we need. Let's heal the world from the endless pursuit of money and power, and re- centre our values."

Everybody was fully engaged in the conversation, a conversation that was truly heart centred. These types of conversations allow us to slowly but surely make our way over the bridge to the new world.

The two girls worked at their mother's local restaurant serving fresh sea food and traditional Mexican dishes; a heart and soul family business that has ran for generations. All the locals gathered there weekly, telling each other stories, and valuing a community spirit.

The group chatted for hours more until it was left with only Luca and Guilia, and the full moon beaming above them, reflecting off each other's eyes.

There was at first a silence between them as the others left; a magical silence though, as if their souls were adjusting to the company and the setting they were in. Both nervous, and even though both had enough in them to speak for days on end, the first sentence was a difficulty in the making.

"It's magical here," Luca finally said, disturbing the silence and relieving the nervous tension.

"It is," she replied, looking into Luca's dark brown eyes, seeing the entire universe dance in motion as she did so.

After those words, the conversation flowed late into the night. They talked for hours on end about anything and everything, revealing their entire life stories to each other. Luca told Guilia about the truth of the old man, and his dreams, and Guilia in turn revealed that she herself had felt an entire golden light around her, telling her heart that all she felt was true, and to stick with whatever feels passionately right and true in her heart, and whatever gave her energy and purpose was the truth, and to stick to it. The light embraced her and told her to never lose the purity of her heart. It told her that as long as she stayed true to it her life would work out exactly as she wanted it to. That she would fulfil her destiny. That was the most intensely magical experience she had ever felt in her life so far.

Luca got emotional at hearing her story. They both felt the love. Even though they had only just met. It was the type of conversation and connection that they had both dreamt about their entire lives. A fantasy into reality. A feeling beyond words, because it was the true language of the universe.

Luca had always believed deep within his heart that he would one day meet a girl like Guilia. He had always felt what it would be like without actually experiencing it yet. But now that he had, it was exactly as he dreamt and so much more. This was because before he met her, his heart was reaching into the very soul of the universe where all things are connected, past, present and future, and he had felt what was going to occur in his future; what was already in his heart.

And now, here he was, under the moon and the night sky, in a state that he had never felt in his entire life, a state which no word, no matter how long the word was, could describe. The feeling was the language of pure love. The language in which every single thing on the face of the Earth and into the infinite universe communicates.

Luca and Guilia woke up the next morning in the middle of the beach. They must have fallen asleep in the early hours of the morning after they had their first kiss. People were already out walking their dogs whilst they were still lying there in people's way. They laughed, realising that people were having to walk around them, and that they had fallen asleep right there in the spot where they had that incredible conversation. They both were so grateful to wake up, the sun once again shining its golden light upon them, and explore a full day together for the first time.

The next months were some of the best times that Luca would ever experience in his life. Road trips in Guilia's van, pulling up to stop at some of the best destinations in Mexico. Evenings outside cooking under the stars, the sounds of crickets in the background. They watched heavenly sunrises every morning and walked along the endless sandy beaches, the smell of the ocean and freedom in the air. It was heaven. He had found his soulmate, and one night, they had an important conversation.

They had both talked about their views on life, and their vision for the world before, and as always, Luca was always bewildered by the fact he had met a girl like Guilia, who was like himself; but that night, as they drank a cup of freshly picked Chamomile tea on the roof of the van overlooking the ocean, they talked deeper.

"What do you think your destiny is Guilia?"

"This," she said, smiling.

"What?"

"This; sitting here with you, looking at what the divine has created with love in my heart, drinking this fresh tea we picked today. I know you feel the same."

Luca did, but Guilia continued.

"There are two parts to my destiny I believe. The simple, magical living I just mentioned then; and uniting this world so that all of humanity can experience what they came here to fulfil; passions, dreams, and their own destinies. Of course, also, to balance humanity with nature so we can live alongside our mother once again. I know our destinies our intertwined; you have told me what you went in search for, and what you experienced, and now, meeting me, it's all part of the destiny of the world! I know we are soulmates, and that we need to work together to bring about this time. The time of...."

"Albion" they said together, at exactly the same time!

"How do you know it's called Albion!" Luca exclaimed, baffled!

Guilia though just laughed, knowing by now that synchronicity and destiny work in mysterious ways.

"It really does look like we both have the destiny to unite the land of Albion," Guilia said, and they put their feet up, gazing at the moon in awe, and kissed underneath another blanket of stars, the air warm, and pure freedom surrounding their beings; both engulfed once again in a feeling beyond all comprehension.

Luca really did feel at home in Mexico; his dreams were now reality, and that was only because he followed his heart with courage, flowing with life.

6

chapter

The rest of the world was still in a similar situation as to when Luca left for Mexico three months ago. The ones who were beginning to see the deceptions were starting to get restless. Even though many felt something was off, only few had the courage to speak their truth and actively seek others who felt the same way.

People, like Luca, were also innerstanding that it was not just the 'war' that was planned and staged, but the entirety of reality as many knew it was all built upon lies and deceit. From health, to debt, to law and history, amongst so much more. People were starting to piece two and two together; still the minority, and even fewer could link their knowledge to humanity itself awakening and regaining its sovereignty.

Luca and his now girlfriend Guilia talked a lot about the situation, and how so many people knew bits of the truth, but their conditioning kept them away from mastering the full picture and the nature of our true reality.

"How do you think everybody will finally see through all the lies," Guilia asked Luca one morning.

"I think it can only happen when people start to innerstand themselves and who they are in the grand scale of things; that they have a soul that is exploring this realm to grow and develop. People are on a grand adventure in this life, and when we realise that, everything changes."

"I definitely agree with that, because then people will see that the lies that the controllers have given out simply do not belong in this world of bliss and freedom. Like really, in what reality could pointless war and poor health exist in a world of magic, created by God; it wouldn't, and people need to realise this. I think you can only perceive the truth once you are at peace with the truth of yourself. To be secure in your own humanity is the first step to finding the magic of the universe, and to feel like we do about it Luca. Those that discover the invisible language of the universe will discover that even the so-called 'negative' events are but lessons to learn and chances to evolve. They will see that in everything in this world is that same language, as we are all ONE, with unique, individual souls experiencing this life in a unique way."

Luca was so in awe of Guilia's words, looking into her eyes and seeing what a powerful soul she was. She truly amazed Luca every time she spoke; her energy, her presence and her beauty was utterly enchanting.

Their conversation reminded Luca of the one that he had with the old man back in Bali, and he found himself immensely grateful for the stage he was at in his life. He realised that the same force that ran life itself was guiding him every step of the way in his life so far; from the conversation at the garden centre between the two old women, the sign on the bus, meeting with the old man that came in his dream in Bali; and now, in Mexico, with his girlfriend Guilia speaking about all things destiny.

Tyranny soon found its way to Mexico. It was only a matter of time. Luca, and all the group knew it was coming. There was no way that Mexico would stay the only country in the world with its freedom still intact. None of them knew why it had lasted this far without nothing happening.

Lucianna, Enrique, Jacamo and Francesca all reluctantly stayed at home, whilst Luca and Guilia pondered over the situation in the wilderness of Mexico, staying in the van.

"At least we can just park up in any place we like and stay," Guilia said, grateful they could still stay surrounding by nature in the van, with a good supply of food and water with them to last a while.

Enrique and the others were constantly on the phone to Guilia asking what it was they could do. They just couldn't stay stuck inside when they knew the agenda: total control and elimination of the human spirit.

"I have been thinking Guilia; without the people's consent, the controllers are literally powerless. It is only the people's decisions to comply to what is going on that allows them to continue towards their agenda. The people are incriminating themselves!"

"You are definitely right, but people are so scared that if they go against the rules, they will get in trouble, perhaps even arrested."

"But think about it, if enough people get together, how will they arrest everybody? And I don't mean with useless protests, I mean by enough people saying 'no, I am getting on with my life and I know my freedoms!"

"I don't think there are that many people who are awake and courageous enough to come together though. For me, it seems that there are four types of people. Those that are so lost and so caught up in ego battles, showing off, greedy, and literally oblivious to nature. Then the second group are the ones that believe everything the controllers are saying word for word and are frightened for their lives, neglecting the fact that the real danger is complying to tyranny. The third group see some of the truth but will not act. They are also scared; scared to be wrong, scared they will lose 'possessions,' friends and so on. The fourth group is the one which we are in; the group which will act, especially when uniting with others in the same group. The first, second and third groups will not come together and do anything to fight for what is right; or on the rare occasion, need others to first show them the way and wake them up."

"So really, what you are saying is that we need to get together as many like – minded people as possible before this gets any worse. But how?"

Guilia smiled, "Exactly how we got together!"

Guilia phoned the others to tell them to let as many people as possible know that there will be a huge beach party and a sunset volleyball game on the beach on Friday evening. The plan that Guilia thought up was that if enough people got together, who felt the same, yearning to keep their freedoms, people would see that it was possible to stand up for what is right, alongside the people that you love. By seeing one country stand up, it would create a momentum of trust and belief that would inspire the rest of humanity to do the same, and it would send signals through the invisible collective consciousness that binds all things in this realm to all awaken. Everybody would realise that tyranny is only possible if people agree to it.

Luca knew that Guilia innerstood the way life really worked and was deeply proud to be with her.

Friday night arrived and Guilia and Luca 'illegally' drove to the beach. They had no idea what the turn out would be. They were risking a lot of things. If nobody turned up they would be left exposed to the Mexican police, and reciting natural law might not do the same trick as it did for Luca back home. Even though they knew the law, they would run that risk of being arrested. They had to follow their hearts once more and do what they felt was the right thing to do.

This party was not just any old party, but a means of finding out who was willing to stand up, and to be a lion amongst sheep. It would show the rest of the world that freedom is not something that can be taken away; it is something we ARE.

Luca spotted Enrique and the others; but what he saw behind them, Luca and Guilia were not expecting.

At least one hundred people marched over the dunes of all different ages.

"What did the others do to get all of these people here!" Guilia said, absolutely shocked.

Luca also looked on in astonishment. 'Are there really that many people awake and wanting to fight for freedom?' he thought to himself, speechless.

They all started to walk up to where Luca and Guilia were stood, alongside the van. They were laughing and joking, not looking at all concerned with the fact they were breaking the so- called law. Perhaps they were all so relaxed because they were protected in numbers, or perhaps it was because the sun was shining, and the smell of sea and freedom was in the air.

A man who looked in his late thirties approached Luca, clearly Mexican, wearing a more casual jeans and t- shirt rather than the beach gear of everybody else.

"I guess you are Luca," the man said, speaking good English.

"Yes, I am."

The man pointed to the group and explained that he was a local police officer called Marco. He showed Luca the other three policemen in the group; all of them tall, well-built men, talking and laughing amongst one another.

Luca was temporally worried but relaxed as the man spoke.

"We heard what was going to occur here tonight. We have always known what is going on in the world and with the law to be wrong. We have all been given strict orders to arrest anybody breaking these 'laws' by the ones higher up."

'The controllers,' Luca thought to himself.

"Myself, or my other colleagues over there have never arrested anybody we have seen breaking these mandates. We know our oath, and we respect it and honour it. We will never break it. When we first applied to be policemen we really thought we were working to serve the people; in a lot of ways, we still have, but after having time to think about it, we now realise that who we are working for do not have the people's best interests at heart, it is an illusion."

Luca admired the policeman and the way that he valued his oath above everything else.

"You are an example of what being a policeman should be. Working for the people with honour."

He nodded, and then continued, "If we get caught today, we will lose our jobs for sure, and getting caught is extremely likely. We have been talking seriously to each other though and we were discussing what is more important, our jobs or standing up for what is right. If you listen to your heart, this is no decision. It is the lust for money that has caused people to neglect honour. So many have lost their soul."

Luca liked this man. He knew that he innerstood the language of the heart.

"I know the police force very well. I have been with them for over twelve years. If they see this number of people out, they cannot do anything. What can they do, arrest everybody? No chance. They will make a fool of themselves if they start chasing everybody around. Once I heard about this, I knew I had to come; in unity there is power, and I admire you and Guilia for getting all this together and coming up with this amazing idea."

Luca was taken aback by the policeman's words. Conversations like this made him feel energised, alive and hopeful for humanity. He loved feeling that there were people like him willing to go after what they believe in with courage.

"Thank you so much Marco, I am honoured to have you here. Let's have an amazing night and if we come across any trouble, we will deal with it when it comes."

They shook hands and everybody then helped set up the multiple volleyball courts.

They played through the evening, Luca and Guilia as usual competitive. It was in their nature. The feeling of like-minded people getting together and having a game at sunset was incredible. The feeling of community spirit, new friendships and powerful souls coming together was a magical thing. All of this reminded Luca once again of the old man, and the time he emphasised the importance of building community, making everybody feel loved and important in the world; at times like this the truth and wisdom of the old man really showed itself.

Guilia was also in her element after having played volleyball her entire life. It was difficult for Luca to take being beat by her at times with his competitive nature.

A huge gathering with food, drinks and music was in store after the games. All of them sat in a circle, spread out laughing and sharing stories with the sound of the rolling waves in the background, a fire also crackling strong. Each of them took it in turns to share a story of their visions for the future, and why they had turned up to the gathering in the first place.

Some of the stories that were shared around the circle of equals that evening were incredibly inspiring. Everybody present gained energy simply by hearing one another speak, and the visions that each were feeling were intensified and energised themselves as the group fed into similar visions.

Somebody called Martina said that ever since she was a little girl she had dreamt of a world where everybody was happy. She always wondered ever since why so many were so unhappy and dissatisfied, and why there seemed to be so many problems. She never understood why there were wars and injustices and wanted answers herself, that was what led her to the gathering. When she was younger what seemed like a negative in her parents arguing, actually prepared her for her destiny in discovering why people were so unhappy, and then helping them to find what brings happiness to their hearts. She was now a life coach and writer, and inspired people all over the world to live their dreams. All 'negatives' can be lessons, if you allow them.

Each had their own unique story to tell of why they came. A young man called Mateo said that it was only recently he started to see the lies. It didn't feel right to him that because of somebody else's problems humanity was being forced to suffer as a result.

Sofia, a woman a little older in her fifties, had also gone through life accepting that it was as she had been told, but recently she was awakening to the fact that there was much more to life. It took her longer than some, but she felt it was something to do with the energies in the world why she was awakening, and so many people at once were awakening as well. She felt like a new human ever since the start of 2020. It was now 2023 and the shift was gaining momentum, and the world needed people like Sofia to keep feeling that truth in their hearts and spread the truth as well as living it themselves.

Each story was given full attention by the others in the group, all were extremely intrigued as to what one another was going to say, and how similar it was to their own reason for being there!

At the end of the night, when the last of the people were heading home, Luca and Guilia began to get emotional at what they had achieved simply with an idea and the courage to go through with it. Hearing stories from each soul's journey was an experience unlike any other. Everybody started as strangers with a vision at the start of the night, and at the end were all connected through true, human connection. What a night. This is what the awakening is all about. Laughter, music, and the sound of humans regaining their spirits, their humanity. Laughter and joy feed the earth, they nourish the soil, and it creates a ripple effect that is contagious, echoing out through all the realms so that every living thing is affected. Slowly, slowly, it creates a new world altogether, a world where every age throughout all of time has anticipated. We are our ancestors' wildest dreams. We are the ones we have been waiting for.

The evening drew to a close and there was no doubt that many pictures and videos would soon be leaking out into the world of what happened. Even the ones that didn't have the courage or the awareness to join would be interested in what went on in their town that night. The rest of the police would have also seen what was going on and saw no use in interfering. Perhaps they saw four of their colleagues participating. It would have been extremely embarrassing to arrest fellow policemen for playing Volleyball on the beach. The mission was successful. The ripple effect had begun.

Guilia and Luca continued with the beach gatherings, and the turn out steadily increased, signifying that some people just need other people first to lead the way. Countries around the world started to follow, each of them standing in their power, having seen what occurred in Mexico. Just by Luca and Guilia living their truth and standing firmly in their freedoms, the rest of the world gained momentum. The controllers had no answer, they were frightened; freedom in numbers is impossible to halt.

Police were still being given orders to arrets anybody breaking the mandates, but it was impossible to do; there were too many people now, and too many that knew the true law. Old systems were crashing down, making way for a world of beauty. Do you see; following your heart always leads humanity and yourself to the correct path.

The controllers had no choice but to back down. The restrictions were lifted, but this was only step one. Next was uniting the realm and creating new, fair systems in place of old, corrupt ones; gathering together people of all races and nationalities to work towards the sole aim of unification of the human race.

7

————————

chapter

Luca and Guilia were walking across a path that meandered through an ancient woodland. Lush greenery saturated the area, golden light peeking through the gaps in the leaves, and a relatively wide stream flowed to the left of them. They had the woodland to themselves. Hand in hand, they walked, slowly, an awe walk really, taking in every detail of God's creation. Every sound, every bird, every minute detail; the texture of the bark, the softness of the ground; it was all so sensual. The two innerstood that we were born with these innate senses, blessed with them in fact, so that we could experience the world so intensely. They both felt blessed to be alive; in love with each other, and with life.

A young girl of about eight approached, coming towards Luca and Guilia on the path. It seemed as if she was on her own, but she was only running ahead of her mother and father, as kids do, so full of life and vitality, as it should be.

Luca and Guilia smiled, both of them seeing the truth of life every time a happy child appeared and dreaming about one day having children of their own with each other.

The girl ran up to Guilia and tapped her.

"Hello," Guilia said, "what is your name?"

"Izabella," the girl replied, looking up at Guilia and glancing across at an even taller Luca, her eyes fixated on him for a few seconds.

Guilia looked down at her hands and noticed that she held a piece of paper.

"What would you like to show me Izabella," she said softly.

The girl unfolded the piece of paper, clearly handwritten by Izabella herself.

She spoke, her voice calm but with a hint of shyness in her eyes as she glanced back at her parents who waited about twenty feet away. "I had a dream the other night and I have been trying to find the people who look like the ones that were in my dream. I think that you two look the same."

Luca suddenly became very intrigued by the situation, knowing the importance of dreams, and how they set him forth on the path of his destiny when he dreamt of Bali that time back home in England.

"And what were the people in your dream doing Izabella?" Luca asked.

"They were stood in front of a lot of people and were talking. I am not sure what about. I remember there was a big stone that they stood next to, and then the dream flashed to a script. I wrote the words from the script that I remember seeing on this piece of paper."

Luca and Guilia looked at each other, knowing full well there might be something deeper in this meeting, and the girl's dreams.

"Thank you, Isabella, for telling us this. You have done very well, and you look like a very wise and clever girl. Isabella, what does the piece of paper say?" Guilia asked, taken back by the girl's initiative, but desperate to hear what was on the paper.

"It says that the once and future king shall pull the sword from the stone in the world's time of need. That king will be the man to bring about the age of freedom and restore the greatest world humanity has ever known."

Guilia took in her words but didn't innerstand just yet. Luca however was speechless. He took his mind back to the old man and remembered him talking about this special king. He called him 'the once and future king' also. They were talking about the same man!'

'This all came in her dreams!' Luca thought, this being a lot to take in. 'Why would this come in her dream, why were we in it?' Luca thought, his mind taken back to Bali.

They thanked the girl once more, but she turned around to say one more thing.

"Oh, and one more thing; the time they called it in my dream was something like, Albion."

Luca and Guilia said nothing and just stared at the girl.

"Oh my God Guilia, what is going on! Albion came in this girl's dream, and she had no clue what Albion was or who we were! This is incredible! And she talked about the king the old man taught me about in Bali. He was the king over the world's greatest empire; he desired no power or authority; he served the people and nature only. He told me that this king, he called him King Arthur, was destined to unite Albion again. For her to tell us this and dream about us, we must have a true, big part to play in bringing about this age."

"Luca, this is incredible. She has told us all this for a reason. We need to go over the script and her dream in more detail later. We are being guided so strongly.

That night they both went over what happened.

"Okay, a young girl dreamt about us where we were talking near a big rock. The dream was shifted to a script about King Arthur and Albion and how the once and future king will pull the sword out of the stone and unite the world," Guilia said.

Luca continued, "And she said we were talking in front of a vast crowd of people."

"Like I said before, she has obviously been guided to come and tell us this at this moment in time. Just when we have momentum, and the controllers are hanging on by a thread."

"But what can we do about it," Luca replied, unsure what the next step could be and what the dream really signified.

"Luca, we don't act on things like this intellectually, you of all people should know that. We have to trust, and if our hearts speak to us once again, we must follow them. This cannot be analysed, it just doesn't work like that. It is tempting to analyse things, but life just doesn't work that way.

Luca was once again grateful to have Guilia. Luca and the rest of the world would not be in the position they were in without her. She was a blessing to everybody. Pure of heart, a dedicated, grounded, authentically true human. Just by being herself, she was changing the world, and making a difference to people's lives.

That girl was chosen to show them that script. Kids are not consumed by information and fear. When your heart is open, you channel wisdom and get in touch with the divine plan of all things. The cycle of nature and the natural forces will always overcome anything of imbalance, for example, the controllers.

"They are always looking after us, the guardians, Luca. Throughout our entire lives they have been there, watching over us. I think that kids, because of the way they observe and play to learn things, innerstand our true reality; they see no separation between the imaginary world and the world that we can touch; both are just as real and vital as the other, therefore they can access teachings from the other realities that are trying to guide us, as that little girl did, that is what I think happened."

"It is mind blowing, Guilia. The true reality of our universe is so magical that only somebody with a truly open heart will ever even start to comprehend its beauty."

Luca felt the old man with him, his designated guardian. 'Was it he that showed this vision to Isabella? What is the old man trying to tell me?'

After the meeting with Isabella, Luca began to get emotional when he thought about the journey he had been on, the experiences he had had and the future he was stepping into, a future of the unknown. The feeling of going into the future with total freedom knowing there would be surprises and that life always had his back was indescribable. He loved a life of adventure, of spontaneity; it filled his being with so much passion for life, so that each day he woke feeling excited. Life was on his terms. His life was one, huge adventure; a movie where he was the main character. Since he left for Bali that time, it felt like he and his life were one. He was experiencing himself through the universe and the universe experiencing itself through him. He had discovered the true elixir of life; distinguishing between what matters and what doesn't in one's life. He had given everything to live his chosen life and knew that he was always on the right path when he thought about his life and truly smiled. To be in love with life is the most powerful tool in the entire universe. He innerstood that the number one guardian is the heart. It was his destiny to teach others the language of the heart, so that they too could live a life of their dreams. This is the destiny of the world. His life had been shaped through synchronicity, the language of the world, and he had always allowed himself to be guided by that. It is all about surrendering to the flow of who you truly are. When doubts and 'negative' events occur, it is a chance to learn and develop more. There is no negative, only balance, only yin and yang. None would exist without the other, they work together, exactly the way nature works, as nature is the truth. The only real negative is imbalance, and even that we can learn and evolve from; just as there is dark and light, night and day, sun and rain, magnetism and diamagnetism; negative and positive would not exist without the other. Remember, every single storm ever on this Earth has always run out of rain!

It was yet another soul shaking dream for Luca that initiated the next step though. It was about a rock; a rock that was not the biggest in the world, but it's energy and presence surely was. The engraving on the stone was what stood out to Luca though, even more than the stone itself. It read: 'The stone lies where the challenge is and where you will develop the most, but also where your heart wants to go.'

He woke up. It was still dark. They had camped out in the woods that night under the canopy of leaves and stars above. Guilia was still sleeping but Luca was wide awake now, staring at the night sky, a half, waning moon shining through the gaps in the leaves.

He had not had a dream so intense since dreaming about Bali back at home.

'The stone lies where the challenge is and my heart wants to go. This must be to do with the same stone Isabella mentioned! Where is the challenge? Where does my heart want to go? I know I want to find that stone, that is a challenge in itself, is there anything else that challenges me? My heart likes it here in Mexico, but I can always return if it desires something else for a while.'

Luca was peaceful, lying awake on the floor of the woods, feeling this out and searching his heart to find the answer. It was about a half hour before Luca finally felt what this dream might have meant.

'Wait, the biggest challenge was England! The people were so asleep, not following their hearts at all. That's what pushed me to find a more awakened place. I think the challenge lies back at home!'

He searched his heart, 'does it really want to go back to England?'

Luca loved it so much in Mexico, and he could always return, but the challenge resonated, the land that brought him up and first showed him the beauty of existence he would return to.

'Guilia could always come if she feels like to. I'm sure that she will love to come and see where I came from.' He felt a buzz in his body, a sensation he knew meant he was about to do the right thing.

It was starting to get lighter and Guilia woke to the sound of the birds calling for a new day, as Luca did that time before going to work at the garden centre.

"Luca, how long have you been awake, you are already up and dressed? I just had this dream about going to England where you are from for the first time."

"You are joking! I've been awake for so long because I was thinking about my dream. Well, feeling, I didn't think logically like you taught me. I dreamt of a stone with an inscription saying, 'the stone is where the challenge lies and where your heart wants to go. I was awake feeling out what this all meant. I realised the challenge lies in England and you have just solidified the fact that we need to go there. You dreamt that we should go. Our destinies really are intertwined!"

Once again they were baffled but followed the omens to England. Once you are in the flow, you are in it for good. Guilia was beyond excited to head for where Luca grew up for the first time. Trusting her feelings was now a rhythm, and she was truly dancing in this miraculous dance of life.

They arrived in rainy, cold, dismal Manchester, still with a smile on their faces. How could they not smile? They were living their destinies out. What other greater honour was there?

"You see Guilia, look where I take you, beautiful isn't it?" Luca chuckled, a sarcastic smile on his face.

Luca wasn't actually from Manchester itself, he hated big cities, so crowded and built up, he was actually from a small town called Penwortham about an hour away, and funnily enough, he had only ever visited Manchester once despite living so close.

Returning to where it all began, Luca introduced Guilia to the family. They shared many stories around the campfire that night. There was something primordial about sharing stories around a fire. The fire brings out a sense of peace and a connection to something much larger than yourself, but something that you are also a part of. The fire creates powerful, deeper stories. Our ancestors told stories in this way since the dawn of time itself, and when the dying embers shine, our eyes our fixated on them, creating a warmth in the soul that heals all. It was a long night of catching up, but it was a night up there in Luca and Guilia's finest moments, and they had experienced a lot.

Whilst showing Guilia around the town the next day, a town that couldn't be any more different in character to the ones in Mexico, or Bali for that matter, they stopped in a café for a drink. Outside of the café was an old map of the area and was placed next to the day's specials menu. Luca took a glance. It showed that the nearby villages and towns in the area were once completely covered in water. It showed ancient oak forests, rivers, and streams on the outskirts of the forest. The river had actually been altered from its original course, and the forest had been mostly destroyed, but still had sections of original woodland left. Right in the centre of the body of water on the map was a drawing of a sword with the name, 'Excalibur' written next to it. He stared at the map a while longer, nudging Guilia to take a look. There were a few 'fun facts' at the bottom of the map as well. The one that stood out to Luca was that the body of water that once surrounded the area was the largest expanse of freshwater in the entire country. It was the largest lake in England! They called this place Martin Mere, although on the old map it was named Marton Mere. Luca was fascinated, but then remembered what he had been told about the pulling of a sword from a stone.

"Is this the same sword that we have been told about Guilia, Excalibur, is that the name of the sword?"

"It is definitely possible Luca, have you not seen this map before?"

"No, it just caught my attention then."

"Well, I think that's a literal sign!" Guilia giggled.

They walked into the local library across the road and asked if there were any books or information regarding the history of Martin Mere and the area. There wasn't. The librarian had never heard of the lake or Excalibur. There were no books in the bookshops either, and the internet was void of information. There were one or two books about Excalibur and King Arthur, but none had linked him to Martin Mere or anywhere near the area where Luca was born. The majority believed that King Arthur was a fictitious character.

"So what is all this about on that sign, nobody seems to know a single thing. Whatever it is it is being heavily suppressed. Why have they turned Arthur into a fictitious character when the old man told me he was the greatest king ever?"

"It's probably the work of the controllers, Luca. Do not worry, the truth has a magical power of always coming out, no matter how suppressed it is."

Guilia's words always made Luca gaze into her eyes and wonder just how wise she was.

A couple of weeks later after exploring the area together, they found themselves in the woods near Luca's house having a picnic near the stream. The area was most definitely part of the ancient woodland of the old world. There were dippers hunting on the waters, squirrels spying on them as they laughed and chatted away, dropping acorns on Luca and Guilia's heads. Long- tailed tits played on the hawthorn trees nearby, hunting for what food they could gather in the middle of winter. It was a stunning pocket of woodland, right near Luca's house that he had explored so many times that he knew the area inside out. It was close to his heart, and it nearly brought him to tears coming back there with Guilia. It made much more sense to him now that all the years growing up there had led and developed him for his destiny.

Each tree must have been over 500 years old, one looked over 1000, and they wondered just how much that tree would have seen.

"That tree would certainly know the truth about the land."

"Definitely Luca; do you know, I feel as if I've got a really strong connection to this place."

"Really, in what way?"

"I don't know, I can't explain it, I don't know if it's just because the woods are so magical or if it's something even deeper than that, it feels special."

"They are magical these woods; places like this need to be preserved and honoured," Luca said, looking up at the ancient trees in awe. Thinking about the woods being harmed in any way filled him with disgust.

"There should be a law to arrest anybody cutting down a tree over 200 years old, never mind fake laws with the tyrannous guidelines recently. Do people have any idea how long it takes for a woodland like this to form, literally hundreds of years, we need to grow more and look after the ones we have got left for the future generations. Woodlands are a perfect example of how nature works as one in a completely self- sustainable way. The life force in a wood and the variety of species both microscopic and large is sublime. It truly makes the senses come alive."

"Do you know, Guilia, there is actually a fungus network running deep under the soil that connects all trees together. They communicate their needs, feelings, and state of health, amongst so much more through this network. The ancient trees deliver energy and nutrients to their kin through this but will not deliver energy to something that doesn't belong in the forest, for example, a species from a faraway land. The trees can only thrive in a community. Many experiments were conducted showing that trees that tried growing on their own, separated from the community and fungus network just couldn't thrive. The trees are intelligent beings! They know when harm is about to come their way, they know each other, and they know they need community to thrive; a perfect example as to how humans should live. This was actually all proven, but you can see it clearly just by observing anyway. The ancient trees of the forest are the most important, this is why we must save them. They are the ones that are producing the most energy for the next generation and have the most powerful fungus network. Rhododendron, Oak, Birch, Ash, Hawthorn, Beech, Chestnut, Alder, and all trees that belong to the Celtic tree ogham are vital for the forest to thrive. It is said in some cultures that the true tree of life is actually the Ash tree."

Guilia was so impressed by Luca's passion for the woods and nature, getting inspired herself to do everything in her power to protect nature and what was left of the ancient trees.

A kingfisher then shot across the stream right next to them, it's colours unrivalled in the bird community, it's enchanting, shining blue colour a truly remarkable sight to behold. A kingfisher was always a good omen for Luca after only ever seeing no more than half a dozen in his life, and none were at the stream in the local woods.

They followed the kingfisher's flight next to the stream to get a better view, but it was too fast and they lost sight of it. They noticed though that sat with her back against one of the oak's was a woman perhaps in her late sixties, she was reading, and they didn't want to disturb her so they kept their distance. She was obviously there to have a peaceful, undisturbed morning in nature reading her book with the birds and stream, not to be bothered by two young lovers chasing a kingfisher down the stream.

"If you two are looking for the kingfisher he is on that branch just there a little disguised by that leaf," the woman said, looking up from her book.

"Ah thank you, yes I can see him. I was worried we disturbed you before so we didn't carry on following it," Luca said, seeing that she didn't look too bothered about them being there.

"I have finished the book anyway. I have been watching that kingfisher myself all morning going up and down and then resting on that same branch. I kept glancing up from my book, what a magnificent bird isn't it?"

"It is, it's stunning," Guilia said. "It is a lovely place to just come here and relax. The oak woodlands here are just incredible."

"They were once much larger, this area was once a huge ancient forest, not just a small woodland like it is now. These trees here have lost a lot of brothers and sisters over time," the woman said, sadly, a little distressed herself thinking about the destruction.

Luca remembered the sign at the café.

'So she knows about the ancient woodland!'

The woman picked up her book and put it back inside her rucksack.

"Do you know the book that I was reading actually had some information about this place, it is where I first learnt that this place was once an old ancient woodland. It also has some very interesting facts about the other areas around here."

"Wait, what other type of facts, did it mention anything to do with a place called Martin Mere?" Luca said, excitedly.

"Of course, that was what the main section of the book is about! How do you know about Martin Mere?"

"We noticed a sign at a café the other week with an old map of the area, and on it was Martin Mere and this ancient woodland, and we have been trying to find out more about it ever since, and about the sword, Excalibur." Luca said, with a deep feeling that this woman may know something important.

"Excalibur! Wow you have come to the right place to find out about it, it is all in this book. I will tell you a bit about it and happily give you this book to take home."

"Where did you get the book?" Guilia said.

"It was passed down for generations, we have all read it and my family have all known about the true history of this place, unlike everybody else who lives here. Most people have no idea what this place really was."

Simply by following the attractions in the present moment, which for them was the kingfisher, led them to the next step in their lives which aligned with their soul purposes.

"What is your name by the way?" asked Guilia.

"Marianna."

"Marinna, what a nice name! I was just thinking to myself, we have had so many amazing synchronicities this year, and no matter how many we get they seem to get more and more spectacular each time! What does it teach about Martin Mere then?" Guilia asked, extremely excited.

"Funnily enough, I have just read the last bit of the book that says, 'when somebody wants something enough, especially when it is aligned with their destiny, the universe helps in every way it can. When you are pure of heart and have zero agendas, the world works with you to achieve your dreams and visions.' This is why we have met today. You said that you two have been searching for the true history of Martin Mere and this area. The universe allowed everything to come together, together with the work you put in, as you and the universe must play equal parts, for your discovery of me and the book today. The woods, the kingfisher, your high spirits, me reading by this exact tree and the book all came together so you could achieve your vision. All is one, but all is unique. This is the force that runs all. Great spirit."

"Thank you for those teachings," Luca said, his heart warm and tingly from those words of truth. The truth ALWAYS resonates, that is how you can distinguish between lies and truth.

"It is an honour to meet two young people who are aligned with their paths and connected to nature. I shall tell you some facts then from the book; you two are definitely a part of all this."

"All of what," Luca replied.

"The age of Albion."

"Of course, if we meet somebody like you, you are bound to know about Albion," Luca said, laughing, Guilia too. Yes, we indeed do know about Albion, we are trying to unite it."

"I am not surprised; you look connected, both of you."

Luca told Marianna briefly about what happened in Mexico with the gatherings.

"I knew you were both awake individuals as soon as I saw you. A sparkle in the eyes. It's all in the eyes; and in the way two young adults chase a kingfisher, not many adults do that!"

Luca and Guilia looked into each other's eyes, smiling, seeing the sparkle she meant; they too had noticed 'the sparkle' even when they first met on the beach in Mexico. They then looked at Marianna, she too had two glimmering eyes, the sunlight further emphasising them.

"Where you two are stood now was once a huge ancient forest. Mostly oaks, but there were ashes, beech, sycamore and many other varieties. What is left now is only four or five small woodlands, this one being the largest left where its former glory can still be seen and felt. It was once part of the forest of Lancashire and may even have been connected to the Perilous forest of Cumbria once upon a time.

Luca looked around, seeing that on the outskirts were the other woods, smaller ones, but still with the same huge ancient trees. He grew up admiring the trees and exploring all the woodlands that were left. He hadn't ever really given much thought to the fact that the woods were once connected to one huge forest once upon a time.

"This is the biggest section left by far," she continued. "It was even bigger too this section a couple of years ago back before that hideous, pointless road was built through it, that school, or should I say, conditioning camp, and them awful, soulless houses on that huge estate were built. This landscape has been vastly altered. It was once a massive energy centre, filled with life, an important energetic heart of England, of Albion. The energy can still be felt in these parts of the woods. Over there in the North-east was a huge castle- like structure, demolished and hidden on purpose, it was perhaps one of the finest structures in the entire world, and they only built structures of importance on high energy sights. In the east was a vast network of natural springs which the old world piped in multiple underground systems, still running today, but the controllers are doing their best to hide it from the public. The three springs in the small village of Penwortham alone were st Annes, st Teresas and st Marys, and although they were the Christian names given, they would have had more ancient names previously. All people back then drank water from these springs. They would rather us pay for water that is messed about with than use the purest of all waters. In fact, in the legends, it says that the spring of st Mary has extraordinary healing powers, and the water was rumoured to cure evil just by touching it.

A sacred drinking fountain above another spring, this time in Preston, which they named, 'the dolphin fountain,' was created and used for many years, only for it to be blocked off by the controllers as they do with every sacred drinking fountain in England. It is lucky the spring water still comes through the other pipes. They are hoping people don't discover the spring water coming out these pipes all around. It would for sure raise suspicion.

It really is crazy how they don't want people to drink good water, they don't want people to eat quality foods that graze and grow on the lands, they want people relying on their drugs, their lies, and the system. If people were fit and strong and could look after themselves, they would have nothing to sell us, they would have nothing to control!

Luca and Guilia were captivated.

In the west though, in the distance lies the sight of the biggest freshwater lake in the whole of England. The entire area was once called Martin Mere. The name still stands for a modern wildlife reserve on the area in a small section of the vast area of land the lake once covered, before it was drained through multiple big ditches into the sea. This lake was a sacred lake, an extremely high energetic point in the land, and it influenced the energies and the collective consciousness in the entire realm. This was one of the main energetic points of Albion. The ancestors called this area, the land of Albion. In fact, a very important ley line runs through the area that was once Martin Mere Lake. Ley lines are energetic focal points that run through countries in certain areas. They are also called dragon lines or serpent energies. In the original old world, the ancients built stone circles, tree groves, and Earthworks that were aligned with the celestial bodies on these sights, but sadly, as the old world was destroyed, the majority have been lost, and we now have churches and buildings on these sights that were likely at one point harnessing the electromagnetic energy already prevalent on these sights of high Earth energy. The ley line that runs through Martin Mere is the western line that comes over from Ireland, into England through Saint Annes, across the river Ribble and on to Martin Mere. It then travels to meet all the other ley lines at Arbor low stone circle, a huge Earthworks in the Peak district. Britain, I really do believe is a remnant of Atlantis.

Luca and Guilia looked at each other in amazement. They were learning just how powerful the land of Albion was.

Britain also has the Belinus ley line, or spine of Albion running right through the centre. I tell you now, I have a strong feeling that ancient Britain was and still is the heart of the world. Originally it would have been unrecognisable compared to now. It would have been true old world before the destruction. The Celts and druids were some of the most connected people in history. They placed their wisdom in the stones and ancient monuments where they communicate to all the other ancient monuments and energy centres in the world, just like we are constantly communicating in a language beyond words. The land communicates, that is a fact, it is indigenous wisdom.

Luca and Guilia were learning so much. Marianna was extremely knowledgeable.

Martin Mere was drained about three hundred years ago by a man named Thomas Fleetwood. Apparently, he drained it to create good farmland, and even though there is great farmland there now, I think his motives went deeper. I think the true reason why they went through so much trouble to drain the largest lake in the country was if they were looking for something. Some kind of treasure. Fleetwood went around all four halls in the area that owned a quarter each of the lake in the 17th century. He went to Bank hall, Rufford hall, Scarisbrick hall and Meols hall, and without telling them what he was about to do, began the huge drainage job. It is only pumping stations now keeping the land from becoming a lake again. That is the true history of the land.

"Wow," Luca said, "I can't believe more people don't know about this!"

"They are definitely hiding something," Marianna replied.

The king of that time was the greatest King Albion has ever known, and his wife Guinevere, the greatest Queen. King Arthur is destined to be Albion's once and future king, uniting Albion in its time of need. When Arthur and his wife Guinevere passed away into the other realms, Arthur's sword got thrown into the lake of Martin Mere. A lady's hand reached out and caught it; this was the hand of the lady of the lake to keep it protected until it was needed again in Albion's darkest hour. Merlin then took it from her to place inside a great stone. Since then, it has been foretold that Arthur will rise again to free Excalibur from the stone where the wizard and Arthur's guardian Merlin had placed it to test who would be Albion's greatest leader to take the world into the future we have all dreamt."

Luca and Guilia were in a trance with what she was saying, every part of their being's giving the lady full attention. Goosebumps appeared on their bodies; was this land and the story that they were a part of really that special; it seemed that it was!

Marianna continued, "It is also said that Camelot was actually close to Martin Mere. In the legends, Sir Lancelot, when he was a young boy came to Martin Mere. His parents, Queen Elaine and King Ban had to quickly run away from enemies in France. Apparently, they travelled by boat and arrived on the shores of Lancashire. It was at Martin Mere where Vivian the nymph stole Lancelot and brought him up in the muddy depths of Martin Mere. When Lancelot was ready, he arrived at the court of Camelot, and since then he has been named 'Lancelot of the lake,' and Martin Mere has been called 'the lost lake of Sir Lancelot.' This is all very clear in the legends."

So there it was. The truth about Luca's place of birth. They both felt part of a story, a story written in the same stars that they gazed upon each and every night. They felt part of the awakening of humanity, a part of Albion itself, and they were honoured to be of service to the world bringing about this new time. Luca, above all was shocked that the place that he grew up in had one of the finest legends in the world. Amazing. True high magic.

They thanked Marianna deeply for her time and teachings, always feeling a strong sense of love and purpose when they met somebody with the same vision. It is that coming together of humans as one huge family of brothers and sisters that would make the human race undefeatable to anybody looking to harm or manipulate it.

That night though, as they gazed at the heavens once more, Luca could not get Albion, the lake or the stone out of his mind and just kept thinking about how magical his life was.

There seemed to be a huge split in society all over the world. On one hand were the people that seemed content in the system, the mundane lifestyle and the illusions of freedom that the modern lifestyle brought, and on the other hand were the people who felt freedom in their veins and who knew that there was nothing mundane about life in the slightest. But it also seemed that the first category, those that were stuck in the system, had a division in itself. Like Guilia mentioned back in Mexico, there were many groups of people; some seemed too far gone, their life force completely empty, and some were so incredibly lost in illusions and imbalanced lifestyles that they simply could not handle any change in perception. Some though were stuck in the mundane, repetitive, soul crushing lifestyle sensing something was off, feeling depressed as a result, knowing there was more; their souls yearned for more, but they felt stuck. These types of people were hard to awaken as they struggle to see much hope, but Luca wanted to help so badly, and to let them see and follow the light.

"Guilia, how do we get the people who feel something more but feel pulled back by so many doubts, fears and conditioned beliefs to awaken. These people are suffering needlessly, unable to process the truth."

"We all have our own fears and doubts, some more than others, and some are consumed by them and these are the types of people feeling stuck. This is about the freedom within. We can only guide people to feel this, the rest they must learn themselves. They must learn the lessons their souls need to learn to grow. Once you have freedom within, every single illusion shatters like glass, and once we have the critical mass of the world feeling belief, freedom and hope; every corrupt system on the outside will heal; money, law, health and so on. We will create systems as humans that work with nature under natural law and this way everything will be kept in balance. Our external world is a reflection of our internal world. Our lives are like mirrors. We reflect what we feel. It all starts from within. Just look what we did; we both went through so many lessons and tests to then bring about the freedom we did in Mexico, and then sending the message of freedom out to the rest of the world. We put the work in and the results were transformative. There is hope, the first step is always acknowledging there is hope. People that are greedy, harm nature, harm others and so on will be forced out of the world as there comes a point where nature just will not tolerate any more of these injustices. The balance of the world is steadily being repaired, and us humans just need to help it along the way; it needs to be cleansed from all the imbalances over time. Our happiness, learnt lessons, love and so on help the soul of the world to heal, because humans have damaged her in every way."

"Guilia, can you get any wiser, honestly you are just incredible!"

"Thanks Luca," Guilia replied, flattered. "The energies are working with everybody to push them in the direction of awakening. People are having old thought patterns emerging, old belief systems that do not serve them anymore coming to light and then they are able to deal with them and hopefully heal from them. As the Latin saying goes: Tempora mutantur nos et mutamur in illis, which means when the times are changed, we change with them. The energies in the world are changing, we are going into a new time and humans are changing drastically with the times. The universe is guiding absolutely everybody to be their best self going into this new age, but only few actually hear this guidance. We hear it as we know the language of the world in which the universe speaks in, and that is why we can see life even more magical than a child does; as a child as we know is much more connected to the language of the world as modern, mundane adults are. We are conditioned from a young age to have this language sucked out of us so that a lot can no longer here it. So many seemingly negative events are happening to everybody, but they are not negative, only lessons and challenges; it is the human perception that makes a test or a challenge seem negative, just like what happened to you with Samnal, that was a challenge for you to develop dramatically. The entire world right now is going through its biggest challenge, but if we pass the tests the soul of the world has given to us, we will flow right threw as a collective into the age of Albion!"

Luca could see Guilia getting emotional in a powerful way, she had never spoke so deeply and passionately before. It was as if she was as wise as the old man. Albion meant so much to both of them, and the passion they both felt for their destinies was so strong; they felt the power of all of creation within them, and with that amount of life force, anything is possible.

"Guilia, we are going to do this, we are going to fulfil our destinies!"

And with that they embraced, giving so much thanks to the divine for the blessing of having each other.

8

chapter

L uca, have you heard what has been found in Egypt?" Luca's mother shouted from the window as he was doing a spot of gardening one crisp autumn morning.

"No, what is it mum?"

"Apparently a manuscript of some kind about our reality has been found, it was on mainstream television."

Guilia overheard this whilst sunning herself in the back of the garden, enjoying the last of the autumn rays. 'Nothing good could ever come from mainstream television,' she thought, closing her eyes and relaxing once more.

"Mum, what have I told you about watching the news."

"I just flicked past it and it caught my attention."

"Thats what it's designed to do, catch your attention and distract you from what is true," Luca replied rather irritably, but even he was curious to know what was on this manuscript.

Luca put his shovel down and looked up at his mother. "What does it say mum, I am busy here, it surely cannot be anything positive coming from the controllers," he said, echoing the thoughts of his girlfriend.

Luca's sister, Medea came to hear what was on the manuscript. She too was an awakened individual after having many experiences herself, and was also passionate about uniting the world and bringing about the age of peace, feeling the truth of the world in her being.

She was slightly younger than Luca, and had been away for some time with her dancing. She expressed the truth through dance. Everybody expresses the truth through their own passions and in their own unique way, and now she had returned home to see Luca and the family.

It was so inspiring for Luca to see his sister develop the way she had. She had told him that whilst she had been away she had uncovered so many layers within herself, and Luca could see her soul shining through her eyes. He was prouder than he could ever express with words. Yes, she had been away, but only Luca knew the depths that she was meaning.

Medea, Guilia, Luca and Luca's father listened to his mother about what was on the manuscript.

"Ok everybody, you are not going to like what is said on this manuscript. Apparently in Egypt somewhere near the pyramids inside an old chest a manuscript was found by a group of archaeologists. The manuscript states that this world and in fact the universe is one huge illusion, like a computer program, a virtual reality of some kind. Apparently, a past race in ancient times created the world to enslave the souls of humans; they say that this manuscript dates back 2000 years."

Luca and the others looked at each other, all of them knowing straight away that this was another deception. It didn't feel right at all.

"This must be the last attempt. The last attempt by the controllers to eradicate the truth. We all know that this is a lie, but others I think will buy into this; quite a desperate move by them but also kind of clever. It can never be an illusion this realm; the feelings, the love, the sensations, the magic; one only needs to be connected to themselves to know the truth and see it in every small thing in creation," Luca said. He was so secure in his truth that nothing could shake him off it, he had learnt and experienced way too much to be shaken off track and into fear and deception.

"Exactly," Medea said, "It is like with me and my dancing, I can connect with what's true through that, and it is the feelings and emotions that dance creates for me which allows me to have that connection to life, the dance of life, and myself. It is a magical experience. Humans are only experiencing confusion because they don't have clarity in themselves, but out of confusion surely comes clarity."

Guilia smiled deeply, she had always admired Medea's dancing. "You are both right, I also have experienced the light and the love of what's true, that we are a part of life, and that it flows through us. We are here as infinite beings expressing ourselves in this blissful life." Guilia gazed at Luca as she spoke, remembering all the times they had and the synchronicities all around.

Luca's mother and father looked at them in amazement, inspired by their words.

"We are with you, we don't believe it either, from all the stories you have all shared with us, we are a believer in the world you are trying to build," Luca's mother said, looking around at the three of them and glancing up at Luca's father. "I only wanted to tell you as I feel that it is a very important event for the destiny of the world and I wanted your take on it."

Luca's mother and father had also found more of themselves and had both quit their boring nine until five jobs to follow their dreams, Luca being a huge influence on both of them, inspiring them. They had now started exploring their dreams of the healing arts.

"I wonder what the public will think, I wonder how many will feel what is true rather than think what is true," Medea said, looking around at the nearby houses. "If you just look at anything in nature, be it a bee, a flower, the symmetry on a snail, a fallen tree trunk, or on the fruit you cut open, you can see that God's hand has written all, us included; just look at a fingerprint, every single one is a unique geometric pattern. You can clearly see that the same force that creates fingerprints creates the snail's shell, that is proof that we are all connected! A separation from nature means people are susceptible for manipulation. People have completely forgot about this force. Some people even think that God is only in the sky as a man in the clouds, no, the divine is EVERYWHERE!" Medea was getting passionate; she couldn't understand how anybody could go around day to day and fail to take notice of this force that was in everything in nature.

Luca knew that the manuscript was in fact a half truth. When he looked closely at it he could work out that it was not the world that was an illusion, but the lies of the controllers, the system and the manipulation. The natural world was as real as God himself; it was doubts, fears and a disconnection from self, nature and the divine that was trapping the human soul.

'The controllers always give half-truths!' Luca said, shaking his head.

So many people though were affected by the manuscript. Even those that were awakening now had their doubts about reality. They felt uneasy, disconnected and pulled away from the light, exactly how Luca felt with Samnal back in Bali that time. The old man knew that he had to test Luca in that way for him to develop as a man who was one hundred percent secure in his truth. Perhaps the entire world was going through its own Samnal test, particularly those awakening or starting to awaken; tests of soul are necessary, and the one that the world was now going through was a big one; people felt pulled in so many different directions that they were forgetting to search inside and look at nature. People felt lost; life force was vanishing. The controllers' plan seemed to be working.

'These are the diversions they have created that the old man told me to be wary of, they are everywhere, driving people crazy!'

The manuscript had created a disturbance that only people like Luca were unaffected, those that already had been through tests and felt connected to what was true. The entire world somehow or other had now heard of the manuscript. He felt sorry for the people, he knew how it felt to be pulled out of who you are and to feel but a shadow of your former self; but he also knew how it felt to get that spark in the soul re- kindled and the power and development of character that brought with it.

Luca and Guilia not only now saw faces that were unhappy because of jobs they didn't enjoy, not living their passions and feeling stuck in an artificial society that sucked life force from the people, but they saw faces of people that were starting to awaken and see the light but now looked around with doubts that the world might not even be real at all. Once doubts and fears overcome true feelings you can become a slave to the ones trying to control you. Doubting the world is doubting yourself, who you are and even what brings a light to your heart in life. People were starting to feel a sense of pointlessness, and Luca and Guilia could clearly observe this. Pointlessness is the biggest killer of the human spirit, the worst dis- ease. It deteriorates a human slowly, eating them alive. It was a horrible sight to see for Luca, but he knew that he had to keep faith, that was the only thing he could do. The manuscript was a trap because even if somebody spent years searching for the truth through books, guru's, the internet; they would still never find the truth of themselves; the internal, innate truth, therefore things like the manuscript would destroy the spirit unless faith is kept. This is why it is crucial to search for truth only through the natural world and what feels right within yourself. The true awakened ones were not affected by the manuscript, they, like Luca were trying their hardest to keep faith in humanity and teach others who were now suffering to search within, and that the manuscript was one, huge deception. This was the only true war, a spiritual war, a fight for the spirit. To keep faith was vital, and to never, ever stop believing. Life is learnt from the inside out, not the outside in.

Months and months past and winter was now settling in England. Frost covered the grass and trees and an early morning mist was cast above the fields. The situation was no better, in fact, it was worse. People were stuck inside watching news on the manuscript, wasting their lives away. Programs on the television literally program the mind, and this was clear looking at the people. They had little energy or life force to even go outside on a crisp, sunny day. Luca wondered what the situation was like in the rest of the world. England was always the worst when it came to people living boring, depressing lifestyles, but this had only made it worse, there was hardly a single body out; yes it was cold, but the sun was stunning, the Robins were singing and the frost looked beautiful in- between the trees.

Luca and Guilia stood there frowning, looking into a house where a television was on, a middle-aged woman glued to it, the mainstream news talking about the manuscript again. They were out of view as to not be nosy, but they couldn't help but observe as Luca did all that time ago before he left for Bali, wandering the streets. They shook their heads; a middle-aged woman should be happy, exploring herself, not watching something that destroys all the magic that same woman would have felt when she was a child.

"What would her inner child say to this I wonder?" Luca said to Guilia, feeling upset at so many people's unhappiness. "What can we do Guilia, telling them of the truth doesn't work, I could tell them until I am blue in the face, they just will not listen."

"We need to show them Luca, not tell them."

"But how?"

"I don't know," Guilia replied, a gaggle of geese flying past overhead.

They admired a thrush singing in- between a hawthorn bush, it's call one of Luca's favourite calls out of all the bird kingdom, it was almost tropical in sound. The frost surrounded the thrush and it really was quite a picture with the clear blue skies above.

"We need to find a way to get humanity to feel the truth and the power of nature. Nothing has changed in nature, it is only the perception of humans that has changed. How do we get adults to once again capture the excitement and imagination that their inner child once had, and to make them believe once more?" Guilia asked, thinking deeply.

"I am really not sure, but now look who is thinking," Luca laughed, "feel, not think, Guilia, as you taught me!"

"Let's phone Enrique and the others and ask them how they are and how things are going in Mexico," Guilia said, excited to speak to her friend.

"Enrique, it's good to speak to you, how are you, how is everything going in Mexico, over here in England the situation is bad."

"Hello, Guilia, it is good to hear from you too, I guess you are talking about the manuscript that has been found and the influence it has had upon the population."

"Of course."

"Well, when the news of the manuscript first came out, even myself and the others questioned things and had our doubts, it was such a horrible feeling, but with a lot of talking we realised that this manuscript was coming from the mainstream news, the same channels that promoted the 'war', the channels ran by the controllers, and so things just didn't feel right. We concluded that this was another lie and another step towards their agenda."

"I think it is a diversion off their agenda really Enrique; the 'war' thing failed as a result of what we achieved in Mexico, and now humans are staying within their freedom and power so they needed to try one last, huge thing. We must be known to them, we have been destroying all their plans!" They laughed. "We must destroy this one too somehow. And what about the rest of the people in Mexico, how are they, how are the people at the beach gatherings, the policemen that we made friends with, how are they all taking it?" Guilia was speaking very fast, desperately wanting to find out how her country was getting on.

"Not great, Guilia. Even though many people found out about the lies of the 'war', now they have doubts over reality because of this stupid manuscript. Even though they fought for their freedoms and were half awake, it was quite easy for the controllers to knock them off track, as they nearly did with us. We have taken this actually as an opportunity to awaken further and grow. Really, the ones that are half awake have been affected more than the completely asleep people.

They were feeling excited to be discovering truth, feeling free, and all of a sudden the truth was shattered for them in their own doubts. People who were asleep were already accepting the lies as real before so they didn't have as far to fall, but yes, everybody is still affected here as the rest of the world is."

"Okay Enrique, I kind of anticipated that. Keep faith Enrique, and tell the others to as well, I miss you all; Luca says hello as well, he is waving over here. Bye, hopefully we'll meet soon."

Guilia put the phone down and frowned. "So it is similar everywhere else."

"The controllers have done a good job it seems, Guilia."

"I know, but there must be a way; we need to show the world somehow that all of this is a lie. We need to re- ignite the fire in their hearts. We can't directly tell them as people are at their own stage in evolution and will not innerstand, they need to awaken themselves, but we need to do something that will give them a help in hand, we need to somehow show them that magic still lies in this world and that it is not an illusion, but truly divine!" Guilia said, smiling once more, knowing that all was possible for those that believe.

9

chapter

Luca was once again in the woodland where he had met Marianna, this time on his own. Guilia and Medea were out together and so he felt like going back to the woods to be still and to let answers come to him, perhaps in the whispers of the trees or perhaps in the murmuring stream. He had always called these woods, 'the forest of belief' ever since he was a little boy, and always came to the forest when he needed some time to himself; perhaps it was because he felt the energy, it all made sense now with it being once an ancient forest part of the land of Albion, still holding that ancient memory. He sat still on a fallen tree trunk and just listened; the peaceful bliss he was feeling could never be explained. He knew that having peace of mind was the most important thing, a truly powerful tool. To be truly peaceful in oneself is the key to life.

A tiny whisper came from behind Luca. It spoke his name so softly that he could hardly make out what was being said. "Luca." It came again but still Luca could not see anybody. When it spoke the third time though it was most definitely his name.

"Hello," Luca said, not feeling frightened as such, more confused and honestly kind of excited to discover who could be there saying his name. It didn't answer the 'hello' though.

'Could this be Guilia or Medea playing tricks, but they left to go out together, it can't be.'

He faced the stream once more and heard nothing, but he was no longer able to concentrate on his meditation.

"What did I teach you brother Luca? Nothing, not even an invisible stranger's whisper should shake you off your meditation and peace of mind."

Luca looked up with a jump. It was the old man! He thought his mind was playing tricks.

"Oh my God. OH MY GOD! It is you! What, when, where, how did you get here?" Luca stuttered, astonished to see the old man stood in front of him by the stream in his own lands.

"I wanted to come and see you. I have been watching your journey so far, I am so proud of you; you have embodied all the lessons that we learnt and followed your heart each and ever time it spoke. That takes tremendous amounts of courage."

"Thank you," Luca replied, slightly shaking, still shocked.

'My designated guardian for my journey on Earth,' Luca thought, 'He's seen everything and can be anywhere at any time, I don't even know why I asked him how he got here, it's no wonder he didn't answer properly; if he can come back into his body after being dead for the last 1500 years he can most certainly appear whenever he feels like it!"

"I have seen what you have achieved since our departure; you brought freedom to Mexico and the whole world followed; you met your soulmate, a fantastic gift that this life offers everybody once they follow their hearts, and you learnt of the true history about this place. You have experienced much, but now the manuscript has shown itself, the world is once again in a poor state."

"Why have you chosen to appear at this moment in time, do you worry for humanity?"

"I told you back in Bali that I trust in the destiny of the world."

Once again he chose not to answer Luca's question directly.

"You would only ask that question of me if you yourself did not 100 percent believe in the destiny of the world."

"No, I do, it's just..."

"It's that you believe 99.9 percent Luca. It is only when that number moves to 100 that the destiny of the world can be fulfilled."

Luca innerstood and knew that he must make it 100 percent.

'Wow, his words are just so powerful!' Luca thought, taken aback by the presence of the old man. He seemed to have gotten even more powerful since the first time they met, he had an even stronger glow to him and an even brighter spark in the eyes. After all, we never stop evolving.

"Luca, I think you should follow me."

"Where are we going?"

"Too many questions Luca, not enough trust."

Luca shut his mouth, once more the old man was right.

They made their way through the woods, nearly tripping over the old blackberry brambles from the last summer many times, the woods was surprisingly overgrown for a December morning.

"Today, Luca is the winter solstice, the birth of the new sun. A powerful day indeed. It is the period where the sun stands still, waiting for its re- birth."

"Most certainly, I always make sure that I get out on the solstice and make my prayers."

They carried on walking and came to a gate at the end of the woods, a vast field appeared.

"I thought this field was private, I have never been this far."

"Well, it's not private today, look."

The old man pointed into the distance at the far end of the field where at least a thousand people stood there staring at Luca and the old man climbing the gate.

"What on Earth is going on! Who are all these people?" Luca exclaimed, stunned.

"Once again another question, but in this case I will answer. These people have come to hear you give a speech. Look, there is your sister and your girlfriend stood at the front with your mother and father."

Luca spotted them. He didn't know what to think, he was the most confused he had ever been in his entire life.

'First of all, Guilia and Medea are meant to be out, and where did all these people come from! What is happening!' Luca thought, his mind truly blown.

"How did all these people get here, why are they here really?"

"I just said, to watch you talk. I managed to gather them earlier, that's all I'm telling you."

That morning, the old man had been going around the area telling people that a young man was to give a speech on the destiny of the world and how the manuscript was a fake and a lie. He had told Luca's family and Guilia and even some of his friends what was going to oc-cur the previous week and for them to meet at the field behind the woods on the solstice. Guilia and Medea were told to make them-selves scarce for it was a secret; they didn't even know who this old man was but they trusted his energy, and with him mentioning that it was about the destiny of the world and Albion.

"Come on Luca, shape yourself, they are waiting."

Luca was trying to take it in as he walked slowly towards the huge crowd of people. He felt as if he was dreaming until he saw Guilia's smiling face, his sister, his mother and his father. He saw some of his friends also. He looked behind the first row and noticed that Enrique and the others had come all the way from Mexico! He also noticed Marianna at the left-hand side near the front. He saw some of his ex- colleagues from work at the garden centre, friends from the past when he was younger, distant family members, and plenty of familiar faces that he recognised from his entire life living in the area.

'How on Earth did the old man do this!'

"Okay Luca, breathe, and the field is yours quite literally!" The old man said, trying to get Luca to calm and focus, but he couldn't help but smile at his small joke.

Luca looked at the old man, then at the field of people. The old man handed Luca a microphone. His heart was beating so fast, but it was beating powerfully getting ready for a powerful speech to come out of his soul.

"Presence Luca! Be here now in the moment, rooted to the ground in your body."

Luca's words came up as though he had already planned the entire speech.

"Hello everybody. Quite a long time ago I overheard a conversation between two older women where I worked at a garden centre. They said that the world was about getting by to pay the bills. They said to never take any risks, to live knowing what will happen every day. What kind of a life is that I thought. No excitement, no challenges, no passion, just a boring, mundane life. I said to myself surely, surely this was not what life is about! It played on my mind constantly. I watched as people did the same thing day in and day out. I needed answers. It felt so wrong to me. I saw that nature worked perfectly and beautifully and I saw that humans seemed so lost. What was going on!"

Everybody was captivated by his energy, just how Luca was captivated by the old man's. All eyes and ears were on Luca.

"One night, a dream came to me, and I asked God for a sign of what I should do. It was a magnificent dream. An old man was in it, and he asked me if I wanted to know about life. Of course I did!"

Luca looked at the old man and smiled, he smiled back giving him a gentle nod, and straight away Guilia and Medea had a feeling that the old man next to him was the old man that came in his dreams. Now it made sense to them why the old man had asked them to come. He had told Guilia much about the old man, but she never found out who exactly he was. Guilia smiled and re- gained her concentration on her boyfriend.

"A bus then went past my house. It said VISIT BALI in bold capitols with the same picture that I saw of that magnificent place in my dream; talk about a synchronicity! Straight away I booked my one-way ticket, quit my job and took the flight."

The people were amazed at hearing the synchronicity of the dream and how it appeared on the bus.

"Bali was as beautiful as in my dream and I captured some incredible feelings of oneness, of unity and of connection to God and Mother Earth. It was my full awakening experience, it was magical. I saw everything in nature as one, unique but one. I saw life as bliss and felt ecstatic. I felt the truth. I then met with the same old man that appeared in my dream. He taught me so much. He taught me how important it was to have a connection to yourself and to the Earth you walk upon, he taught me to always stay true to your heart and to always believe in yourself; and he also taught me about the controllers that run the systems of the world through fear, dividing humanity and sucking it's life force, telling lies; the same controllers that have created the manuscript that you all fear and believe. Do you see, you are all in fear, that is what they want. He told me of the plan of the made up 'war' and of the endgame of total control of the population. He taught me about Albion and the once and future king, the great civilisation that King Arthur created; that he was not a king as we know as he desired no power, only freedom. Then, I was tested when I met a man called Samnal. He tested my will and my soul with a test that made me question everything, even my own true feelings, my beliefs, and all the old man taught me. It threw me into fear and doubts, exactly like everybody else in the world is in now; what you are all in right now. It was much needed though as I came out resilient, strong and firmly in my truth, THE TRUTH, unshakable in it shall I say."

Not one voice was heard out of the thousands but Luca's, it was as if the people were in a trance.

"I arrived back here in England facing the tyranny of the controllers, it was so horrible. Tyranny all based on lies surrounding a completely fake narrative. I broke the so- called 'laws' many times by doing something as innocent as going for a walk! I knew though that I couldn't stay here in England, I needed to find somewhere that was free where I could find like- minded people who wanted to work towards the same goal of freedom and truth. I followed my heart to go to Mexico where I had the time of my life and achieved so many of my dreams and hearts desires. There, I met Guilia, my soulmate."

Luca pointed at Guilia who had Medea's hand on her shoulder. Luca and Guilia both had tears in their eyes. Luca wiped them and carried on.

"She is the most beautiful, wise, determined and passionate girl I have ever known, although my sister Medea would probably have something to say about that!"

They all laughed, tears still streaming from Guilia's eyes.

"Her belief in herself and the world has inspired me on a level that I never imagined I could feel. We thought up a plan to destroy the tyranny in Mexico; we got together hundreds of people with the help of friends that I made who are here with us today and went against the 'laws'. There were too many of us to deal with for the police, so they had to leave us be, in fact, some of the police actually joined us which was heart-warming to see them standing up for what was right! What a night it was, and it was a night which gave momentum to the rest of the world to stay within their freedoms. The collective consciousness felt what we did, and news spread fast; the people felt true freedom in their hearts that they had never felt before. They felt a new spark of power.

We then had a meeting with a little girl who also had a dream of her own about a script explaining that only the true king of the world would free a sword embedded in a great stone; I came back here after that, after myself and Guilia both had dreams that we knew signalled to come back here. All things are connected, and so we followed the omens once more. We came here and met Marianna who I can see in the group with us today also; she taught us so much about the land we are stood on, how it is the land of Albion, and that a huge lake once surrounded the nearby area where King Arthur's sword, Excalibur was thrown before it was taken by Merlin where he thrust it into a great stone.

Now we are here, humanity suffering because of another lie from the controllers. The manuscript is their last chance to enslave humanity. Look around, how can this be an illusion. Search your hearts, feel the sunlight on your skin, the Earth on your feet; feel the love from your friends and family, your passions sending electricity through your veins. This is what is real! Do you hear that Robin singing? He doesn't care that a manuscript was on the news, he already knows without a doubt that life is created by great spirit, and he lives as a spiritual being having an experience as a Robin to the best possible level. We humans need to live also to the best possible level in this incredible world that God has created for us. It is a crime to take it for granted. We are a part of this. No manuscript is the answer, no knowledge is, no Guru is, no external factor is. Being human is though! To be sovereign, to be authentic, to feel what is true; to not listen to anything that feels wrong; it is a lie, it is as simple as that. Break out of the illusions, the true illusions. The world is not the illusion, your fears are! Set yourselves free! Set yourselves free with the inner knowing that you are a spiritual, infinite being that is living a temporary experience on this absolutely stunning Earth. How can anybody even consider this Earth to be an illusion? Look at its beauty, look at the beauty within yourselves, how nature works together; we are nature! The manuscript is a fraud to suck your life force. Once you stay firmly connected to the authentic expression of who you are, your individuality, your uniqueness, you will fly, I am telling you! Feel the magic, see the lies. Be YOU, live your passions, follow your dreams. WE ARE FREE. THE AGE OF ALBION IS HERE!!!"

Luca finished the speech, his whole body tingling all over from the passion and the energy he was producing; his soul was on fire and the old man was smiling deeply. The audience was silent, simply in awe of Luca's words. Everybody was trying to innerstand what was being said; their hearts were saying, 'he is right, listen to him,' but their brains were struggling to keep up because of the mounds of conditioning and indoctrination over the years they had been alive by the controllers, their own fears and their own doubts. Still, deep down they innerstood, and their hearts had come alive, soon they would have to choose between what their hearts told them or what the conditioned brain said. They were all in the presence of truth.

Everybody felt the energy and it was unlike anything any of them had felt before, especially being stuck in a state of fear for far too long. Guilia ran up to hug Luca, in tears; his sister Medea soon joined him as well as the rest of his family, they were all extremely emotional. The audience talked amongst themselves about what was said, there was no applause, it wasn't an act, it was pure truth; it touched everybody so deeply, and the truth was starting to give a nudge to everybody present to awaken. Nobody just suddenly awakened though, it didn't work like that, but they felt the hope, and that was the first step of awakening. They picked up on Luca's passion. Positivity and love are contagious forces, and Luca had given everything that he had in that speech. Spontaneous speeches from the heart are always the most powerful.

"So everybody, words of wisdom there from a young man who has found the truth by listening to his heart. Luca has been on an extraordinary journey, and it is not over yet, there is still one other thing that he wants to show you all," the old man said, loud enough so everybody in the audience could hear.

'What does he mean, surely my speech was enough! I have given everything I have in that speech, I know they felt it and were beginning to innerstand, what else does he want me to do?"

"Luca, follow me. Everybody follow me!" he shouted, and the people wondered what was going to happen next. A lot had already changed for them, they had been inspired and felt new light in their lives, but yet they were still to follow the old man, for something else was to occur.

He made his way towards another gate that led into yet another part of the ancient woodland, the solstice sun was now shining bright on all their faces, low down in the winter sky. Everybody followed the old man through the gate.

The old man stopped a couple of feet into the woods and turned to face the thousand people behind him. They all stopped themselves anticipating the old man to speak.

"Where you were stood before on that field was once the largest freshwater lake in England, Martin Mere. King Arthur, the greatest king this land has ever known had his sword thrown into the water upon his passing from this realm. A hand reached out from the lake and caught the sword as it was thrown. The hand belonged to the lady of the lake, and down it went into the depths of the sacred body of water where she protected it until Merlin asked to take it from her to get ready for Arthur's return into the realm in Albion's time of need. He took the sword into the nearby ancient woodland, the same woodland that you are stood in now and thrust the sword into a great stone with all his power. He prophesied that only the true king of the world would be able to pull the sword free from the stone and unite this realm once more. Merlin was ready for the new age that was dawning; he felt the energies, he believed in the world and believed in his own destiny 100 percent. He also believed in the destiny of Arthur upon his return, and he waited until the day would come where the sword could be freed from the stone with excitement. The stone still lies untouched today with Excalibur still stuck inside, waiting to be released."

The people were once again captivated, talking amongst each other about the legend. Some had heard about King Arthur, Merlin and Excalibur, but none had known that the legend lied in their own town! Some had lived there all their lives and not one of them knew of the story surrounding their lands, all there was was a sign outside a café in the main street of the town; a sign that only Luca and Guilia noticed, and that played an important part in the destiny of the world.

"Behind the great oak lies the sword in the stone," the old man said, so calmly it was as if something like that happened to those people every day! The old man pointed and walked towards a gigantic oak, at least 1500 years old, it's trunk as wide as six people stood next to each other.

The people talked amongst one another, their hearts all beating fast; the ones that had heard about the sword in the stone had thought it merely to be a myth, but none would ever dream it was for real, never mind be placed where they lived. They couldn't believe what was happening.

They followed the old man, Luca closely behind him, whispering to Guilia what in the world was happening.

"I'm in shock Guilia, it can't be, I must be dreaming!"

"You said you wanted to find the stone Luca, and it looks like it's here!" Guilia said, smiling. She didn't seem as shocked as Luca, it was like she expected to find the stone, and this was because she had unshakable faith and trust. She was still mesmerized however by the majesty and size of the huge stone and the sword in front of her eyes. The stone was about three meters wide and one meter high stood behind the largest tree she had ever seen. The most beautiful sword in the world was wedged inside. It had gold engravings on the blade and a gold top with the words 'take me up and cast me away' on the blade itself. Ancient symbolism could be made out along the top of the blade which was as sharp as any weapon Luca had ever seen. The sword glimmered so brightly in the solstice sun, emphasising the polished gold on top of the handle and the Celtic engravings; talk about presence! It wasn't just the sword that stood out but the stone itself, both had the sun's rays illuminating them, every single eye was drawn to the sword in the stone like a magnet. One single ray came from the sun and shone right through the bare trees so it hit the top of the gold handle of the sword, as if the sun itself knew what was happening and was pointing to the sword. It was the God ray. It was truly the most beautiful scene anybody there had ever witnessed. The great oak, the sun, the bare silhouettes of the winter branches and the Robins made the occasion truly heavenly. Enchanting was the only word to describe the scene.

"Guilia, is this real or am I dreaming, pinch me!"

"Luca, you are not dreaming, this is your destiny, the destiny that we have been a part of together. It has only just begun."

Luca's family, friends and all the other people stared at the stone, also wondering if they were dreaming. Hardly anybody spoke, this was not the time to speak, every soul was coming alive and witnessing true magic in front of their eyes. Magic is here every day, but this time the people just had to acknowledge it.

"Luca, look at me," said the old man in a different voice than Luca was used to hearing, a much more powerful voice from the depths of his soul, sending goosebumps through his body, "You are going to pull that swords from that stone."

"What! You have got to be crazy, pulling a sword with my bare hands from a solid stone. It's well and truly embedded inside! Surely you don't think I am the true once and future king!"

"Luca, you are not; but you will be once you pull that sword out of the stone."

"It is impossible, I am still only human, maybe you could but I could never...."

The old man interrupted Luca. "It is not my destiny to pull that sword out, it is yours. If you don't believe, you are no different than the ones who think they are powerless in an illusionary world; Luca, you can do it, there is no such word as can't, you'll do well to re-member that. Look at what has happened in your life so far; the syn-chronicities, the love, the magic; why do you believe in them but yet do not believe you can free that sword?"

Luca paused, he forgot that he had a thousand eyes looking at him, he was trying to innerstand what the old man was saying.

"Everybody! Luca here is going to pull this sword out of the stone to prove to you that magic still exists in the world and that all you have to do is let hope into your heart and believe. He is going to prove to you all that he is the once and future king!"

"You've just told half the town that I am going to free this sword from the stone!"

I know, because you are."

"How!"

"No questions brother Luca, feel with your heart, not with your brain."

Suddenly, Guilia's words came back to him, how he should always feel and never think about matters that concern the heart, the brain cannot comprehend these things. Guilia spoke pure truth, and just hearing her voice inside of him gave him strength, but he now needed to find his own inner strength.

Luca placed his hands on the glimmering gold handle of the sword and straight away felt it's power. He felt that it was created by the same hand that had created all in the universe. He felt Guila's power with him, he felt Excalibur's power, but he still needed to find his own power to complete the sacred triskelion. He pulled the sword slightly, feeling that it was so embedded inside the rock that no ordinary strength would ever have a chance to pull it out. The blade was at least a quarter inside the stone. He closed his eyes and tried to believe but nothing happened. He felt he looked stupid trying to pull a sword out of a stone with his bare hands with a thousand people watching. His hands were shaking like crazy.

"Guilia," the old man said, "come and stand on the left of Luca and I'll stand on his right."

Feeling Guilia now with him gave him strength and he felt the love from her and his family watching. He once again tried to believe but the sword still didn't move an inch.

"Luca, 99.9 percent is not enough, what did I tell you. You must believe 100 percent without a doubt in yourself that you will pull the sword out." He spoke slowly to Luca, making sure that his soul took in his words.

All at once, every single event happened in his consciousness, he felt the awakening at the lake in Bali, his first kiss with Guilia, his passing of the Samnal test. He felt all the synchronicities and the moments he felt truly alive with his heart alight. He heard his own speech from earlier, 'It is your own fears and doubts that are the illusion!' Feel the magic, see the lies. Be you, live your passions, follow your dreams. We are free. The age of Albion is here.' His eyes glowed and he tightened his grip on the sword. He felt Guilia's hand on his shoulder and the presence of the old man. He heard himself from the past, 'this cannot be what life is about!' He then felt the experiences that he had with Guilia in Mexico. 'That is what life is about,' he thought, the energy now pulsating in his body. 'There are no limits! The only limit is YOU!' He believed 100%, his hands were shaking no more.

As soon as he felt that one hundred percent belief, the winds started to pick up, as if the divine and Mother Earth herself felt Luca's belief. It was the highest wind, coming from the very soul of the world, blown down from the heavens, touching everybody present. Great spirit had manifested itself as the wind to witness the miraculous event that was about to occur. Only those that innerstand the language of the soul can ever make it to the highest wind.

Luca's veins were just about exploding with energy, his inner strength incomprehensible. With that, he lifted the sword out of the stone, tears in his eyes, the sun rays sparkling on the blade and on Luca's face. He stared at Excalibur in the beauty of the setting solstice sun. He held it there for a minute, feeling the moment. PRESENCE. He then hugged Guilia, almost suffocating her. The vast crowd of people cheered like they had never cheered before; they were feeling emotions that came from the very deepest part of their soul. They were witnessing the destiny of the world unfold before their eyes. Luca's family ran up to him, everybody was ecstatic, the energy through the roof. The winds were still blowing strong, only adding to the aliveness of the occasion.

Every single being there would never even dream of something like this happening, never mind happening in real life; they were bewildered. They turned to each other just to make sure that it wasn't just them imagining it. Enrique and the others were so spellbound by what happened, smiling so deep within their hearts, their own friends achieving something so great; and being a part of this filled them with pride, as it did for Marianna. Luca's mother and father and Medea ran up to Luca and Guilia, tears streaming down their eyes. What a magical story was unfolding; a story that simply wouldn't be without anybody who had a part to play. Everybody in the world plays their own part, their own melody to the collective song that is the song of life that we all dance to each and every day. Luca and Guilia were dancing right in the centre of it that day though, and every single being's hearts had never felt magic like it, they were in the presence of pure love, the power of the infinite.

When things calmed down a little Luca shook the hand of the old man.

"Thank you, thank you for everything brother."

Everybody soon took a minute to themselves to take in how incredible what happened was. It had given people belief, the most powerful force. Nobody was forced to awaken, but they had seen something so magical that their hearts expanded hugely. What everybody witnessed that day at the stone though could be felt by gazing at a single flower head. The same magic that was in the pulling of the stone was everywhere in creation, because remember, great spirit writes all. God believed 100 percent without a doubt in himself, so creation was brought about; Luca believed 100 percent in himself so the sword was freed, and so anybody can believe 100 percent, so anything is possible.

The crowd took it in turns to congratulate Luca and headed home completely different people than who arrived. Word got out to the world about what happened, the controllers knew they were defeated.

The people had hope, they had belief, and the world found out that the manuscript was a fraud.

Luca and Guilia talked all night like little kids on Christmas eve. What a day!

"I always knew that we'd succeed!" Guilia said, a huge smile on her glowing, pretty face.

"So did I, but when I first got to the stone, all my fears and doubts returned; but the belief that I managed to find in myself was unlike anything I have ever felt before! What does that mean now, that I am the King, that I was Arthur in my past life?"

"I suppose so," she laughed, "but not a king who rules, a king who slowly creates fair systems for the world so that everybody can be themselves, living their dreams; but also a king that still wants to travel around Mexico and further, living simply with me and the van! And one day we can have a family of our own who we can teach all these lessons to. What amazing kids they would turn out to be!"

Luca laughed. "Wait, if I was Arthur, you must have been Guinevere! You always said that you had a connection to this place."

"I think I might have been, wait, sorry Luca, I FEEL I might have been!"

They laughed once more; it was the most powerful day any of them had ever had and would stay in their souls for eternity.

"We've got a lot of re- building to do in this world to balance humanity once again with nature," Luca said, finally feeling tired after the exciting day.

"But we'll do it, 100 percent."

The next morning, Luca and Guilia greeted the sun that was now on its journey into spring after the solstice, and thanked life for everything like they did every morning, but even more so now.

There was a knock on the door they heard whilst they were cooking breakfast.

"One of my fans I suppose, Guilia!"

Guilia giggled.

Luca opened the door.

"Hello Luca, congratulations again for yesterday. I always believed in you 100 percent as I believe in the destiny of the world 100 percent." It was the old man!

"Thank you, brother. Thank you for everything, the guidance, the lessons, even the harsh ones, you are a blessing to everybody," Luca said, surprised as ever to see the old man.

"As are you brother, Luca. There comes a time though where even though we are brothers and sisters, and I do like being called 'brother,' that one must know my true name."

"You are finally going to tell me your name!"

"Yes, Luca, my name is Merlin."

"I should have known!" Luca laughed. "Merlin the magician! The magician who took Excalibur. Since we met that day in Bali you have always known what my destiny was!"

"I have known a long time before that Luca brother, and I always believed in you!"

"What a journey I have been on. I have to pinch myself that this is my life! You have been guiding me every step of the way since I was born. I will always remember you brother; you are a true friend."

"As are you Luca, you are one of a kind. I have loved every step of the journey and every conversation we have had, and I will continue to guide you now that you are King. Our journey will live long in the world and will inspire people throughout every age."

"Well, Merlin, it has been an honour and a privilege to work with you and to have you in my life. What should I do with the sword now I have it?"

"First of all, call it by its name, Excalibur, I named it. Keep it somewhere close to you, it's power will help you shape the world we have all longed for. But promise me something, Luca. When the sword's job is complete, you must throw it back to the spirits of Martin Mere. The lady of the lake will look after it for eternity. Give me your word, Luca."

"I give you my word, Merlin! It would be my pleasure."

"Thanks, Luca, our word is our bond."

"I know where I will keep it for now though; in Guilia's van, then it will come everywhere with me!" Luca said, laughing. "When will I see you again?"

"Whenever I want to pop by and have a cup of tea in that van of yours!"

They laughed their heads off, Guilia hearing them from the kitchen, wondering who he was speaking to.

"There is one final gift that I want to give you Luca brother."

"Oh please, you have done enough! What more could there be to give?"

"When somebody offers you something you must take it Luca. This is a gift directly from my heart to yours, one I hope you will remember me by and use in your visions for the future."

He gave Luca a bracelet. It was a bronze bracelet with two dragon heads facing each other, signifying the age of Albion.

"These two dragons Luca are the two dragons that guard the land of Albion. They are slowly awakening along with the rest of humanity. The two dragons have slept through humanity's darkest hours and now are now being called out into the light once more as a result of your hard work Luca. You deserve this bracelet. Wear it with pride now that you are King. One day the two dragons will once again roam our world freely just like humans will be free. They are the sacred gatekeepers of our world, Luca, the sacred gatekeepers of Albion."

"Thank you so much Merlin, honestly, I am eternally grateful! How is it that every time you speak you give lessons and share interesting stories?"

"It's just one of my many talents Luca, my destiny."

They laughed. They had both loved each other's infectious presence, and they both had a deep connection, a soul connection. Just like the bee and the flower back at the garden centre, they both needed each other, they both wanted each other, but they had unique destinies which worked towards the ONE destiny. Just as Luca didn't have the magic that Merlin had, Merlin could not pull the sword from the stone. Each had their destiny and their part which only they could perform. The bee can produce honey, but only because the flower allowed itself to be pollinated. Both the bee and the flower though, worked towards the same vision.

"Luca, I have also got a special gift for Guilia."

The old man reached inside his rucksack and pulled out a cup, an ancient looking cup, quite large, also bronze.

"This Luca is the cup of life," he said, like everybody pulls one out a bag every day!

"The cup of life! You are not serious are you!"

"Of course, I can't give away Excalibur without giving away his sister the cup of life, so I thought who better to take the cup than Guilia. Luca, tell Guilia the legends about drinking it for immortality are not true. They always hide its true purpose. As you know, this realm is a temporary realm; we are not meant to be immortal in this physical body; our souls already are. The cup of life and Excalibur are symbols, symbols of belief, of hope, of pure love. They are physical manifestations of these symbols. The truth always tends to get muddled up, no doubt the controllers had something to do with that. Keep them together Luca, they love each other, just like you love Guilia. People have guessed at the truth since the dawn of time, but without heart centred knowledge they will never find it, nor find Excalibur or the grail. Guilia is a pure heart, worthy of the grail"

"Well, what can I say! I'll tell her you bought a pair of shoes for her and then she will have a big surprise when she unwraps it!"

They both laughed so much, Luca now getting used to holding some of the world's most sought-after objects; and with that, they said their goodbye's; their destinies were intertwined, just as Guilia's and Luca's were, and everybody they met along the way. There are never any chance meetings. All is written. Just stay in the flow. Luca saw Merlin off down the driveway; he got into no car, he simply vanished at the end of the driveway, and all Luca could do was smile. "What a life!"

"Who was that?" Guilia asked.

"Merlin."

"Merlin!" Guilia exclaimed, "is that the old man then! He has known about you all this time since he came in your dream, incredible. This life is so full of wonders that only when we search for our destinies can we perceive them!"

"Guilia, Merlin bought you some shoes."

"Shoes! Oh, he didn't have to; are they magic shoes?" Guilia said, laughing.

Guilia unwrapped 'the shoes.' "What on Earth, it's a cup! What is this Luca?"

"Okay, okay, it is the cup of life."

"THE CUP OF LIFE! He has given me the actual cup of life! I'm lost for words. People have been searching all over the world for this and he has kept it all along to give to me when the time was right, and Excalibur to give to you. Just think about it Luca, we have met Merlin, you pulled EXCALIBUR from a stone, and now I have the cup of life! What kind of sorcery is this!"

They laughed so hard whilst having some eggs on toast with Excalibur and the cup of life sat on the table with them. Who would have known it, the same Luca who worked at the garden centre would embark on such an incredible journey by following his heart and end up with Excalibur, the love of his life and the cup of life sat with him. Truly, anything in life can happen. One thing is for sure; Merlin knew all along.

Luca and Guilia resumed their life on the road in the van and Luca's family moved in with Guilia's family in Mexico, innerstanding the importance of community. Luca headed off in the van into the sunset, Guilia by his side, and an open road in front of him was all he ever needed. Simplicity, that is the answer. They parked it up by the beach and took off their shoes, their feet touching as they walked across the warm sand, hearing the waves coming closer. A lovely breeze touched their faces, or perhaps it was the spirit of Merlin telling them they had truly reached the highest wind as the very last of the sun was fading into the endless west. The prophets that spoke of the time of the sixth sun were correct; it was a new age, a new beginning, and the air itself smelt of a purity that signified the shift had happened. They had made it to the other side. They had manifested the vision that had always been in their hearts. Once again the magic they saw in everything had yet again increased tenfold. They loved the simple life and wouldn't change a thing. Remember, when you keep it simple, you get life.

"I'm sure every day just keeps getting more and more magical!" Guilia said, with so much gratefulness in her heart.

"It certainly does Guilia. I love this realm with every ounce of my being!"

They gazed at the setting sun that was exiting the part of the realm for the night and saw the moon come up behind them. They reached for a blanket and sat there with some drinks and snacks, listening to the waves. Birds were flying away to rest for the night, the sea shimmering below them. The sand was deep orange with the last of the sun's rays and they took it all in. Every ounce of it all soaked up into their beings. What more can you ask for out of life?

10

chapter

Over the years, Albion was born. What was once simply a vision; a dream, was now reality for Luca and the world. Slowly but surely, all the corrupt, unjust, disconnected systems and deceptions crumbled, making way for new, harmonious systems. This was only possible because the people started to believe in themselves, in who they are, and in the fact they are a free soul living a human experience, creating community, friendships, love, laughter and facing many challenges for growth. The people started to believe because Luca and Guilia showed them that anything was possible once belief is kept 100 percent. They showed them that yes, the pulling of the sword from the stone was magical, but that anybody can find that same magic in themselves and anywhere they look.

The building of Albion didn't happen overnight, it started way before Luca was born; in fact it started from the birth of the Earth itself. Everything up to this point in history had been leading up to it, creating pathways for it to be born, and it will also continue to build for a long, long time. Awakening is not something that happens overnight; it takes time and a lot of patience, but the results are finding the true you and why you came down here to live in the first place.

When Luca was in his past life as King Arthur, he had tried his best to unite the world just as he had done as Luca, but greed soon enough took over and humans once again lost their essence. This time though that wouldn't happen again. The once and future king had now united the lands forever, and the people now had true connection to the Earth and themselves. The energies in the world were different now, and the people were now working with them with unshakable faith that could never be broken. All the generations that would follow, and then the children of them, would each solidify and enhance the ways of freedom and sovereignty. What Luca and Guilia managed to achieve with the world would create an upwards spiral that would constantly evolve. Every thought, every action, every deed, and every single thing you do has an impact on every generation.

There still were people left behind in the old ways, but that was fine as well; each individual soul has its own unique journey to find its purest expression and is at a different stage in its evolutionary progression. For everybody there is always hope to see the light. The light is there for all, we all just need to follow its shining golden rays. Just as the old man said, each soul is exactly where it needs to be. Even in the time of deception, humanity at some level chose to be in that situation. It served them in the moment, but through deep healing and awareness, humans can consciously choose to set themselves free. Regardless of what situation you find yourself in, the universe is ALWAYS working for you. We are safe. We are always guided.

The age prophesied since the dawn of time was beginning, the people truly uniting, and nature was innerstood as the one, true guide. Truth ALWAYS overcomes lies. The journey that Luca and Guilia had been a part of, and all the ones they met along the way would go down in history, the true history, and be remembered through every generation until the end of time. Is there a more honourable gift than leaving a fair, free world for the forthcoming generations?

Never again would the world be taken over by any form of controllers, for even they would begin to heal and make amends. Once humans are truly connected, they will never lose that connection. The destiny that the world had been waiting for ever since time began had arrived. Luca and Guilia never thought of the significance of their journey when they first began, and that allowed them to follow their hearts, and look where it has led them; to uniting the world, both of them fulfilling every single one of their soul ambitions. Finding each other and living simply in their little van with nature being one of the biggest ambitions fulfilled for their souls. Remember the different purposes the old man gave when it comes to living life!

Luca and Guilia looked around at what they had created and saw that humans were working in co-operation with each other, just like nature had always done and continued to do. Humans now innerstood the importance of each individual to the whole, and each were aligned with the authenticity of their soul, working as one with the soul of the universe. A united world speaks the language of the heart, and when that happens, no division could ever take place again. What can be divided when we are all ONE?

Don't forget, the awakening isn't complex. Simplicity is the answer. It isn't rigid. One being awake could mean somebody who lives their passion of surfing or dancing every day, another might find the divine through yoga or travelling. Some incorporate many things. There is no right way as the old man taught when it comes to finding the divine. The only lesson is in your own heart!

Trees were planted all over for the next generations and ancient forests were preserved. Wildlife gardens flourished all over the world. Nature was honoured, it was respected, it was one with humans. All systems were built on the principle of honour. The law was natural law only, do no harm, cause no loss, injury or damage to anybody or their property. Electricity was free and clean, produced from electromagnetism, working with our world to produce it. Communities were formed, in fact, the entire world was one huge community; divisions between countries were lost and ways of life respected. Soil health was respected, the sacred springs were honoured and re- built. It was a united world, a United Kingdom. War was unheard of; the controllers had vanished. People lived their passions, their dreams and gave their unique service to the world. The truth was being brought out fully; it was truly a heaven on Earth. Imbalances were healing, people were innerstanding the way health works, and the way life works. They were connecting to themselves, to nature, to great spirit. Smiles were around every corner, smiles that came from the heart and not faked. Emotions were felt and not repressed. Traumas were healing, and people were finally feeling ALIVE. It was the AGE OF ALBION. Luca and Guilia had built what they had always dreamt about, they had followed their hearts, they had followed their destinies. Luca wasn't treated like a king, nor Guilia a Queen, but like friends, as equals, as it should be. After all, they still lived in a van, albeit one that was now running off the electromagnetism of the world so they didn't have to keep stopping for petrol! They were still the same Luca and Guilia that met on the beach all those years ago; they never forgot who they were, and why should they, as all they ever had to do was BELIEVE.

AND ONCE YOU FIND THAT 100% UNSHAKABLE BELIEF; YOU TOO CAN PULL THAT SWORD FROM YOUR VERY OWN STONE.

James Valerio Caggianelli

James is a writer, speaker, adventurer and film maker. He has a huge passion for writing, expressing divinity through his words, and has done ever since he was a young boy. As said in his book, you know your true passions and talents when looking back on your childhood thinking what gave joy to your heart. It is what gives you passion and purpose.

He is the co- producer with AMANI STUDIO PRODUCTIONS of 'PROPHECY OF ALBION' a documentary out now on Youtube, James' channel being 'theageofALBION'. The prophecy of Albion is a four hour long film covering subjects on sacred water, sacred springs, the true ancient world, the life/ death cycle, King Arthur and the truth about North West England, Native American wisdom, the destruction of the old world, The eagle and condor prophecy, amongst much more. Incredible visuals and music. Some say the best documentary on the subjects in recent times.

On his website www.jamescaggianelli.com is his course 'YOU ARE THE POWER'. A deep course on how to embody true health, aliveness and vitality and use the knowledge of the heart to uncover the truth about who you are and the truth about life itself. Highly recommended for anybody wanting to know themselves on a deep level and actually integrate feeling truly alive in daily life.

YOUTUBE: theageofALBION
Instagram: ageofalbion
website: www.jamescaggianelli.com

Also check out James' sister, Athena's incredible poetry book, 'THE NOURISHED SOUL' 'You just open a page and it hits you exactly where you need it'

www.ingramcontent.com/pod-product-compliance
Lightning Source LLC
Chambersburg PA
CBHW051455050726
47593CB00005B/2090